CRIMINAL JUSTICE
IN MICHIGAN

ELLEN G. COHN
Florida International University

PEARSON
Prentice
Hall

Upper Saddle River, New Jersey 07458

Executive Editor: Frank Mortimer, Jr.
Assistant Editor: Sara Holle
Production Editor: Barbara Cappuccio
Director of Manufacturing and Production: Bruce Johnson
Managing Editor: Mary Carnis
Manufacturing Buyer: Cathleen Petersen
Creative Director: Cheryl Asherman
Cover Design Coordinator: Miguel Ortiz
Cover Design: Denise Brown
Cover Image: Day Williams/Photo Researchers, Inc.

Pearson Prentice Hall™ is a trademark of Pearson Education, Inc.
Pearson® is a registered trademark of Pearson plc
Prentice Hall® is a registered trademark of Pearson Education, Inc.

Pearson Education LTD.
Pearson Education Singapore, Pte. Ltd
Pearson Education, Canada, Ltd
Pearson Education–Japan
Pearson Education Australia PTY, Limited
Pearson Education North Asia Ltd
Pearson Educaçion de Mexico, S.A. de C.V.
Pearson Education Malaysia, Pte. Ltd

10 9 8 7 6 5 4 3 2 1
ISBN 0-13-114031-0

CONTENTS

PREFACE

This supplementary text will provide you with specific information on the Michigan criminal justice system and the Michigan criminal law. Throughout the text, you will find quotations which have been taken verbatim from legal documents, such as the Michigan Compiled Laws and the Michigan State Constitution. Any misspellings or other irregularities are reproduced exactly as they appear in the original documents.

I hope that you enjoy this supplement and find it both interesting and informative. If you have any questions, comments, or suggestions, please feel free to contact me via email.

Ellen G. Cohn, Ph.D.
cohne@fiu.edu

CHAPTER 1

THE STATE OF MICHIGAN

INTRODUCTION

Michigan is located in the Great Lakes region of the United States. It is made up of two peninsulas that together border on four of the five Great Lakes. The lower peninsula is much more heavily populated and industrial while the upper peninsula contains more unspoiled wilderness regions. The capital of Michigan is Lansing and the largest city is Detroit. The state bird is the robin, the state animal is the whitetailed deer, the state flower is the apple blossom, and the state tree is the white pine. The state's nickname is the Wolverine State.

THE HISTORY OF MICHIGAN

Michigan Before the American Revolution

Most of the early Native American population of Michigan belonged to three main Algonquian-speaking tribes. The majority lived in the lower peninsula and were primarily agricultural. These included the Potawatomi and Ottawa tribes. The Ojibwa (also known as the Chippewa) lived in the forests of the upper peninsula and depended on hunting and fishing for survival. Other smaller tribes found in the region included the Menominee, the Miami, and the Wyandot.

The first European to reach the Michigan region was the French explorer Etienne Brule, who reached Lake Superior in 1618. Although his original purpose in exploring the area was to locate a water route to the Pacific Ocean, he promptly claimed the region for France and was followed by other French explorers, traders, and missionaries. In 1668, Father Jacques Marquette founded a mission at Sault Sainte Marie, on the upper peninsula. This was the first permanent settlement in the region. Explorations of the region continued and additional missions, military forts, and trading posts were built in both peninsulas during the next 30 years. Fort Pontchartrain was established on the Detroit River in 1701. This eventually became the city of Detroit. French interests in the Michigan region focused on the development of the fur trade and the conversion of the natives to Christianity. A small number of French inhabitants established farms along the Detroit River.

Between 1689 and 1763, the British and the French fought a series of four wars in North America in an attempt to gain control of the continent. The last of these, the French and Indian War (also known as the Seven Years' War), lasted from 1754 to 1763 and ended with the signing of the Treaty of Paris on February 10, 1763. As a result of the signing of this treaty, Britain gained the rights to all French territories east of the Mississippi River, including French holdings in the Michigan region.

The British actually took over French settlements several years before the signing of the Treaty of Paris, beginning with the occupation of Detroit in 1760. Like the French, the British focused primarily on the fur trading opportunities to be had in the Michigan region, rather than creating farming settlements. Although these activities did not greatly affect the Native Americans already living in this region, British colonists moving into the regions that would later become Ohio and western Pennsylvania did force Native Americans from their ancestral lands. In addition, many of the natives had supported the French during the wars and resented the presence of the British. Anger towards the British led to a 1763 rebellion by an alliance of Native American tribes led by Chief Pontiac of the Ottawa tribe. Members of the alliance attacked fourteen British forts and posts and captured ten of them, killing many British settlers. The attack on Detroit was led by Pontiac, who laid siege to the fort for over five months. However, after France signed the Treaty of Paris, ceding the region to Britain, they refused to provide assistance to the natives and the attack on Detroit was defeated. In 1765, Chief Pontiac entered into a formal peace treaty with Great Britain.

Shortly after the end of Pontiac's War, Britain placed Michigan under the control of the province of Quebec. However, the British government's focus on fur trapping and trading led it to deny Britains the right to purchase land in the region as a way of discouraging settlement and protecting the forests necessary for the fur trade.

Michigan During the American Revolution

Detroit was a key region during the American Revolution. British raiding parties used Detroit as a base from which to attack American settlements in the region. Mackinac Island, a small island in northern Michigan which housed a British fort built in 1780, was another British stronghold during the war. In 1783, with the signing of the Treaty of Paris (not to be confused with the 1763 Treaty), the American Revolutionary War came to an end. Under this treaty, control of the present-day Michigan region was ceded to the United States. However, the British continued to maintain control of Detroit and Fort Mackinac in the hopes that the new nation would fail and they could continue the fur trade in the region. It was not until 1796 that the United States took control of Detroit and Fort Mackinac after the signing of Jay's Treaty (named after the American statesman, John Jay, who negotiated the treaty with Great Britain).

Michigan As a United States Territory

In 1787, the United States Congress passed the Northwest Ordinance, creating the Northwest Territory. Much of what is now Michigan was included in the Northwest Territory after the signing of Jay's Treaty. In 1803, the entire Michigan region became part of the Indiana Territory and in 1805 Congress passed an act that created the Territory of Michigan. The capital of this new territory, which included the entire lower peninsula and a small eastern portion of the upper peninsula, was

Detroit. President Thomas Jefferson appointed General William Hull to be the first governor of the territory.

In the early 1800s, less than 4,000 white settlers lived in the Territory of Michigan, most in the areas of Detroit, Sault Sainte Marie, and Mackinac Island. The settlers focused on supplying the needs of the fur traders who worked in the region. The War of 1812 significantly affected the Michigan Territory. The country that controlled the region also controlled the Great Lakes so Michigan was a focus of the war and several key battles were fought there. Detroit and Fort Mackinac were captured by the British in 1812, before news that war had been declared ever reached Michigan. The Americans recaptured Detroit in 1813 after the Battle of Lake Erie but several American attempts in 1813 and 1814 to recapture Mackinac Island failed. The war ended in 1815 with the signing of the Treaty of Ghent. Under the terms of this treaty, Fort Mackinac was returned to the United States.

After the War of 1812 ended, population growth in the Michigan Territory was slow. This was primarily because it was not located on the primary routes used by pioneers moving westward. However, the completion of the Erie Canal in 1825, which linked the Great Lakes and the Atlantic Ocean, created a new route for settlers moving to the western territories from states in the northeast. Many settlers, especially those coming from New York and New England, chose to stay in Michigan and purchase land in the region. Michigan's population increased from approximately 31,000 in 1830 to over 212,000 in 1840. The heavy concentration of New England settlers had a significant influence on the development of Michigan as a territory and a state.

Michigan As a State During the 19th Century

According to the Ordinance of 1787, before a territory could become a state, it must have a population of at least 60,000. Michigan's population reached this point in 1834 and the following year a constitutional convention was held and a constitution adopted. On October 5, 1835, the constitution was ratified by the people and Stevens T. Mason, the acting governor of the Michigan Territory, was elected the first state governor. However, Congress did not immediately recognize Michigan as a state because of a boundary dispute between Michigan and Ohio. In 1836, Congress settled the issue by giving the disputed land (a strip of land near Toledo) to Ohio and giving the Upper Peninsula region south of Lake Superior to Michigan in compensation. On January 26, 1837, Michigan became the 26th state in the Union, entering the United States as a free state. The capital of the new state was Detroit.

The Constitution of 1835 is considered by many to be the state's best constitution. One of the most significant elements of this constitution was an article dealing with education that provided for a superintendent of public instruction to serve as a member of the executive branch of the government. The article also created a fund for the support of schools within in the state.[1]

After Michigan's entry into the Union as a state, immigration continued to increase. British, Germans, Irish, and Dutch immigrants all arrived in large numbers between 1830 and 1860. Most chose to farm areas in the lower peninsula but large numbers of miners from England, primarily Cornwall, settled in the upper peninsula. As a result of the development of the mining industry in Michigan (especially iron and copper ore), the Soo Canal was completed in 1855. The canal allowed ships to pass between Lake Huron and Lake Superior, giving the miners a way to ship ore out of western Michigan. The forest regions of northern Michigan also led to the development of a thriving lumber industry in the 1840s. In 1847, the state capital was moved to Lansing. A new constitution was adopted in 1850. It was more than twice as long as the 1835 constitution. Key provisions of this constitution included:

- making the offices of secretary of state, attorney general, auditor general, and supreme court judge elective, as a way of limiting the power of the state governor

- requiring that the question of a general constitutional revision be submitted to the voters of the state in 1866 and every 16th year following

- ordering the establishment of a state agricultural school[2]

In 1854, the first Republican party in America was founded in Michigan. The party was formed to oppose the extension of slavery in the United States. As a result of its New England heritage (many of the first settlers in the region were originally from New York and New England), Michigan was strongly abolitionist and an important stop on the Underground Railroad.

Between 1861 and 1865, Michigan supported the Union during the American Civil War. The Fourth Michigan Cavalry was responsible for the capture of Jefferson Davis, President of the Confederacy, in Georgia on May 10, 1865. General George Armstrong Custer, who led the Michigan cavalry during the war, was probably the most famous resident of Michigan to serve in the Union Army. One Michigan woman, Sarah Emma Edmonds, fought with the Union Army disguised as a man.

After the end of the Civil War, increased immigration into Michigan led to the continued development of agriculture. The lumber industry also increased in importance and by 1870 Michigan produced more lumber than any other state. Detroit became increasingly industrialized and its manufacturing output continued to grow rapidly. Between 1870 and 1890, the population of the state more than doubled and the state began to develop a fledgling tourist industry as well.

Michigan During the 20th Century

Between 1854 and 1932, Michigan was primarily a Republican state. During this time, the state had only three non-Republican governors and one Democratic U.S. senator. In the early 20th century, Michigan became a key state in the Progressive movement. Important governmental changes that occurred in Michigan during this period included direct primary elections and direct elections for U.S. senators, the use of the initiative and the referendum, and the establishment of workers compensation programs. In 1908, the state adopted a new constitution.

The creation of the automotive industry around the turn of the century had a major impact on Michigan, eventually making Detroit the capital of the automotive industry. Ransom Eli Olds and a group of Lansing businessmen founded the Olds Motor Works in Detroit in 1897. In 1901, they created the first automobile assembly line and began mass-producing the Curved Dash car. In 1903 Henry Ford founded the Ford Motor Company and began producing the Model T in 1908. Ford established one of the first profit-sharing programs in 1914 and paid a minimum wage of $5.00 per day, at a time when skilled workers earned $2.50 per day and unskilled workers $1.00. As a result of the development of the automobile industry, the population of Detroit increased rapidly, becoming the fourth most populated city in the country by 1920 with a population of approximately 1 million. The state as a whole became significantly more urbanized and industrialized. During World War I, the factories turned from automobile production to the production of armored vehicles, trucks, airplane engines, and other products needed by the military. Despite the existence of a chapter of the Ku Klux Klan in the state, large numbers of blacks moved to Detroit from the south during the war, looking for employment opportunities.

The Great Depression greatly affected Michigan during the 1930s. Because few people could afford automobiles during the economic downturn, the state's unemployment rate soared, with several hundred thousand workers losing their jobs. Federal employment programs such as the Civilian Conservation Corps and the Works Progress Administration employed many Michigans during the Depression. One result of the Depression was to break the domination of the Republican Party on Michigan politics. In 1932, the state supported Franklin D. Roosevelt for President and elected Democratic candidates to the majority of state offices.

In 1935, automotive workers in Detroit founded the United Automobile Workers of America (UAW). As major automobile manufacturers refused to recognize the union, workers held a series of sit-down strikes in the plants. In December, 1936, the UAW went on strike at the General Motors Plant in Flint, locking themselves in the factory and demanding recognition by General Motors, a union shop, and the right to collectively bargain. The strike ended in February, 1937, when the union was given collective bargaining rights for the workers. The UAW was recognized by all other major automotive companies except for the Ford Motor Company, which did not allow union representation until 1941, after an employee strike at the company's main plant.

During World War II, automobile factories again converted from automobile production to the production of military equipment such as tanks, ships, and airplanes. Wartime production helped bring about a return to prosperity in Michigan. Workers came to Michigan from around the U.S., drawn by the jobs in the military plants. Many of these were blacks, migrating up from the South. As during World War I, they faced racial tensions and discrimination. In 1943, racial tensions in Detroit resulted in a riot that left 34 people dead.

The factories returned to the production of automobiles after the end of the war. An increasing demand for cars, trucks, buses, and other vehicles encouraged more workers to move to the state. The mining industry also began to revive during this period and a new copper mine opened in 1955. Between 1950 and 1960, the state population increased by 23 percent.

The Democratic Party continued to gain strength in Michigan after the war. G. Mennen Williams, a Democrat, served as the state governor from 1949 to 1960, for a total of six consecutive terms. He was the first governor ever to serve more than three terms in the state. Democratic support from black voters and organized labor allowed the Democrats to win the majority of statewide elections during the 1950s. The Republican Party retained control of the state legislature during this period.

A recession in the United States in the late 1950s significantly affected automotive production and sales, resulting in increasing unemployment in the state. The industry began to prosper again in the early 1960s as automobile purchases increased once again. However, as a result of the recession and the rising costs of social welfare and other public needs, Michigan enacted a flat-rate income tax in 1967. This allowed for increased spending for government services such as education, welfare programs, and mental health facilities.

Between 1908 and 1961 a total of four attempts were made to revise the 1908 state constitution. In 1961, a constitutional convention was convened with a total of 144 delegates. The proposed constitution was adopted by the convention in August 1962 and approved by the voters in April 1963. It went into effect in 1964.[3]

During the 1960s, the state suffered from a variety of racial and economic problems, especially in the inner-city areas. As residents moved out to the suburbs, the cities experienced increasing problems of unemployment and crime. A riot in primarily black neighborhoods in Detroit lasted for eight days in July, 1967. Violence, burning, and looting left forty-three people dead and resulted in the damage or destruction of approximately $45 million of property.

Crime continued to increase in Michigan during the 1970s and 1980s. The state also continued to experience racial tensions. Federally-mandated desegregation of public schools was strongly resisted by whites in Detroit and other cities. Tensions between whites and Native Americans also increased during the 1970s as members of Michigan tribes demanded that the state government honor earlier treaties. In 1979, a federal court decision upheld the rights of the tribes to hunt and fish in traditional areas in the state.

During the 1970s, many automotive plants relocated from urban areas into the suburbs, or to other states, creating more unemployment, neighborhood decay, and increasing crime. The 1973 Middle East oil embargo, which caused gasoline shortages throughout the country, led to a decrease in automobile sales and further injured the automotive industry and the state's economy. Tourism, another important industry for the state, was also hit hard by the gasoline shortage.

The first black mayor of Detroit, Coleman Young, was elected in 1973. Gerald R. Ford, a Michigan native, was appointed Vice President of the United States in 1973, after the resignation of Spiro T. Agnew. He became the 38th President of the United States in 1974 after President Richard Nixon resigned in the wake of the Watergate scandal.

The state's economy began to improve in the mid 1980s as automotive sales began to increase again. The government ordered a temporary increase in the state income tax to allow the state to restore funding that had been cut from various educational, health service, welfare, and other statewide programs.

In 1983, James Blanchard became the first Democrat to hold the governorship in 20 years. He served as governor for ten years, until his defeat by Republican state senator John Engler in 1990. Engler's economic and fiscal reform package eliminated the state's $2 billion dollar deficit and created a $1 billion surplus in five years. Unemployment reached a 20-year low and the state lead the country in new business growth by the middle of the 1990s. Engler's reforms included changes in tax laws that encouraged business growth and reduced individual property taxes, the privatization of various state services, and major welfare reform.

Today, Michigan's economic dependence on the automotive industry has been reduced significantly. Other important industries include the manufacture of computers, communication equipment, and high technology devices. The service industry is also important to the state's economy, as is tourism.

MICHIGAN TODAY

Michigan is the 11th largest state in the country, with a total land area of 56,804 square miles, as well as 38,192 square miles of Great Lakes waters and 1,704 square miles of inland waters. Slightly over two-thirds of Michigan's land area is made up of the Lower Peninsula, which measures approximately 285 miles at the widest north/south point and approximately 195 miles at the widest east/west point. The maximum distances in the Upper Peninsula measure approximately 125 miles from north to south and approximately 320 miles from east to west. Until the two peninsulas were connected by a five-mile bridge over the Straits of Mackinac in 1957, the only link between them was a ferry service. The average elevation of the state is approximately 900 feet above sea level. The Michigan shoreline is 3,288 miles long; only Alaska has more shoreline. The state borders four of the five Great Lakes: Lakes Erie, Huron, Michigan, and Superior.

Currently, Michigan is the 8th most populous state in the country. The 2000 census[4] reported a total population of 9,938,444, an increase of 6.9 percent over the 1990 figure. The population density of the state was 176 persons per square mile. Approximately 26 percent of the population were under the age of 18, and 12 percent were 65 years or older.

The most populous city in the state is Detroit, with a population of 951,270 in 2000. Other cities with a population of over 100,000 include Grand Rapids, Warren, Flint, Sterling Heights, Lansing (the state capital), Ann Arbor, and Livonia. Wayne County is the largest county by population, with 2,061,162 inhabitants in 2000.[5]

According to the 2000 census[6], approximately 80 percent of the state's population are white, 14 percent are black, 2 percent are Asian, and 0.6 percent are Native Americans. Slightly over 3 percent of the population are reported as being of Hispanic or Latino origin, although they may be of any race. Only 5.3 percent of Michigan residents are foreign born, less than half the national figure of 11.1 percent.

Michigan has a total of 83 counties, each governed by a board of commissioners. The state elects two United States Senators and 16 members of the House of Representatives, for a total of 18 electoral votes. The current state constitution was adopted in 1964.

NOTES

1. Michigan Legislative Council (2002). *Michigan Manual, 2001-2002.* Lansing, MI: Legislative Services Bureau.
    (http://www.michigan.gov/emi/0,1303,7-102-116_355-2838--,00.html)
2. *Ibid*
3. *Ibid*
4. United States Census Bureau (http://www.census.gov)
5. Census and Statistical Data for Michigan (http://www.michigan.gov/census)
6. United States Census Bureau, *op. cit.*

CHAPTER 2

INTRODUCTION TO MICHIGAN CRIMINAL LAW

THE STRUCTURE OF THE GOVERNMENT

Michigan criminal law is found in the state constitution and in the Michigan Compiled Laws. Both have been frequently modified, amended, and altered over the past 150 years.

The current **Michigan Constitution**[1] was adopted in 1963. There have been three earlier constitutions, adopted in 1835, 1850, and 1908. The Michigan Constitution is the primary law of the state, although it is of course subordinate to the United States Constitution. No criminal law or constitutional amendment enacted in Michigan may conflict with or violate any individual rights which are guaranteed by the U.S. Constitution, the Bill of Rights, any other Constitutional Amendments, or any federal laws. If any part of the Michigan constitution or legal code is found to be in conflict with the U.S. Constitution or federal statutes, the Michigan enactment is unconstitutional and must be changed.

Article XII of the Michigan Constitution, entitled "Amendment and Revision", discusses the various ways in which the constitution may be amended or revised. First, an amendment to the constitution may be proposed by the state legislature. If the proposed amendment is agreed to by a two-thirds vote of the members of each house, it is submitted to the voters of the state for ratification at the next general or special election for majority approval. If a new or revised amendment is ratified, it goes into effect 45 days after the date of the election.[2]

Second, a constitutional amendment may be proposed by voter initiative, via petition. The petition proposing the amendment must be signed by a number of registered voters that equal at least ten percent of the total number of votes cast in the last general gubernatorial election in the state. Amendments proposed by petition are presented to the voters at the next general election and must be approved by a majority of the voters. Ratified amendments go into effect 45 days after the date of the election.[3]

Finally, the voters may call for the formation of a constitutional convention to revise the state constitution. Beginning in 1978, and every 16 years after that, the voters decide whether to call for a constitutional convention. If a majority of the delegates elected to, and serving as, members of the constitutional convention support a proposed constitution or amendment, it is presented to the voters of the state for majority approval. If ratified by the voters, it will go into effect on a date prescribed by the convention.[4]

Like most states, Michigan has three branches of government: executive, legislative, and judicial.[5]

The Executive Branch

Article V of the Michigan Constitution discusses Michigan's **Executive Branch**. The governor, lieutenant governor, secretary of state, and attorney general are elected by the people at a general election and serve four-year terms.[6] In 1992, the electorate voted to impose term limits on certain elected state officials. As a result, the four elected executive officials are limited to two terms in office.[7] These terms do not have to be consecutive. Other members of the executive branch, including the treasurer, are appointed by the governor with the consent of the state senate.[8] To be elected to the offices of governor or lieutenant governor of Michigan, candidates must, at the time of election, be at least 30 years of age and have been a registered voter in the state for the preceding four years.[9]

Among the powers and duties of the state governor is the "power to grant reprieves, commutations and pardons after convictions for all offenses, except cases of impeachment, upon such conditions and limitations as he may direct, subject to procedures and regulations prescribed by law..."[10]

On November 5, 2002, Jennifer M. Granholm, a Democrat, was elected the 47th governor of Michigan. She took office on January 1, 2003 and is the first woman to hold this office in the history of the state. Her present term expires in 2006 and she may be re-elected to one additional term of office.

The Legislative Branch

The **Michigan Legislature**, which is discussed in Article IV of the Michigan Constitution, is the lawmaking branch of the state government. The Legislature is made up of two houses: a 38-member Senate and a 110-member House of Representatives. The Legislature meets annually in Lansing. Senators are elected to four-year terms (which are coterminous with the governor's term of office) while members of the House of Representatives are elected to two-year terms. To serve as a member of the Michigan Legislature, an individual must be at least 21 years of age, a U.S. citizen, a qualified voter in the district s/he represents, and have no convictions for any felony involving a breach of public trust within the past 20 years.[11] In addition, individuals who are government employees or officials are not eligible to serve in the state Legislature. The only exceptions to this are notaries public and members of the U.S. armed forces reserve.[12] State senators may serve a maximum of two terms and representatives may serve a maximum of three terms.[13] These terms do not have to be consecutive. The lieutenant governor of Michigan serves as the president of the Senate, although s/he has no vote in the Senate except as a tie-breaker.[14]

The duties of the Legislature include enacting the laws of the state of Michigan, proposing constitutional amendments, and levying taxes.

The Judicial Branch

The judicial branch of the government, which is discussed in Article VI of the Michigan Constitution, contains the various state courts. The highest court in the state is the **Michigan Supreme Court**, which has seven members who are elected by voters at a statewide election and serve eight-year terms. *One of the justices is selected by the court to serve as the chief justice.*[15] Only the U.S. Supreme Court may reverse a decision of the Michigan Supreme Court. The state's intermediate appellate court is known as the **court of appeals**. It is composed of 24 judges who are elected to six-year terms.[16] Michigan's trial court of general jurisdiction is known as the **circuit court**. Each of the 56 judicial districts in the state has one circuit court. Circuit court judges are elected by the voters in their districts and serve six-year terms.[17] Courts of limited jurisdiction in the state include probate courts, district courts, and municipal courts. The Michigan court system is discussed in more detail in Chapter 5.

Passing a Law in Michigan

In Michigan, a bill or proposed law may be introduced into either the Senate or the House of Representatives.[18] According to the State Constitution,

> No bill shall be passed or become a law at any regular session of the legislature until it has been printed or reproduced and in the possession of each house for at least five days. Every bill shall be read three times in each house before the final passage thereof. No bill shall become a law without the concurrence of a majority of the members elected to and serving in each house. On the final passage of bills, the votes and names of the members voting thereon shall be entered in the journal.[19]

The courts have held that the requirement of reading the bill is satisfied if merely the title of the bill is read aloud.

After the bill is introduced into one of the legislative houses, it goes to the first reading. The title of the bill is read aloud and the Speaker of the House or the Senate majority leader refers the bill to a standing committee. The committee studies and debates the bill and makes a recommendation regarding approval. The committee, or any member of the Legislature, may also recommend or propose amendments to the bill. To move out of committee, the bill must be approved by a majority vote of the members of the committee. The bill then receives a second reading. At this time, the full membership of the legislative house or origin considers the recommendations of the committee, debates the bill, and has the opportunity to offer amendments. During the third reading, the bill is open for further debate and voted upon. Passage of a bill requires a majority vote from the members of the legislative house. After the bill is passed by one legislative house, it must go through the same procedure in the other house. If amendments are made, both houses must agree to the changes.[20]

After a bill passes both houses of the General Assembly, it is ordered to be **enrolled**. A clean copy, containing any amendments is prepared and sent to the governor. The governor has fourteen days to review the bill and consider his or her actions. If the governor approves and signs the bill, or if s/he fails to veto it within fourteen days, the bill will become law. If the governor vetoes a bill, the Legislature may override the veto by a two-thirds vote of the members of each house.[21]

THE MICHIGAN STATE CRIMINAL LAW

There are several sources of criminal law in Michigan. These include:

- federal and state constitutions
- statutory criminal law
- common law
- case law

Together, the Michigan Constitution and the U.S. Constitution provide the basic framework for criminal law, first by focusing on individual rights and on the limitations placed on government power and second, by requiring the establishment of a judicial system. However, neither the federal nor the state constitution significantly emphasizes the creation or definition of crimes.

The primary sources of **statutory criminal law** in Michigan are Chapter 750 (Michigan Penal Code) and Chapter 752 (Crimes and Offenses) of the Michigan Compiled Laws (MCL).[22] However, other statutes also contain laws which relate to crime and punishment. For example, Chapters 760 through 777 make up the Code of Criminal Procedure. Chapters 701 through 713 comprise the Probate Code, which deals with the treatment of juvenile offenders. Other chapters deal with topics such as search warrants[23] and the rights of crime victims[24].

The Michigan Compiled Laws were originally based on the English **common law**, which became the law of the original thirteen colonies and then evolved into the law of the individual states as they entered the union. The common law developed out of common customs and usages that developed over a very long period of time. Statutory law is based on these common law principles. Article III, §7 of the Michigan Constitution states that:

> The common law and the statute laws now in force, not repugnant to this constitution, shall remain in force until they expire by their own limitations, or are changed, amended or repealed.

Because of this, state courts may use the common law to analyze and interpret the state's criminal code. If a specific crime is not defined in the statutes, the common law definition would be applicable. However, if a statute supercedes the common law, that statute becomes the controlling law for that issue.

Case law consists of appellate court decisions or opinions which interpret the meaning of the statutory and common law. Effectively, case law is made by judges when they hand down decisions in court. Because of the principle of ***stare decisis***, or precedent, a decision made by a judge in one court will be followed by later judges in the state until the same court reverses its decision or until the decision is overturned by a higher court. According to the Michigan Court Rules (MCR), for an opinion of the court to be binding under the rule of *stare decisis*, it must be published.[25]

The Michigan Compiled Laws contain two types of statutory criminal law: substantive and procedural. **Substantive criminal law** includes definitions of specific crimes and identifies the punishments associated with each criminal act. MCL §750.316, the section of the Michigan Penal Code that defines first degree murder, is an example of substantive criminal law. **Procedural law**, on the other hand, focuses on the methods that are used to enforce substantive criminal law. In other words, procedural law outlines the rules that the state must follow when dealing with crimes and criminals. These include the procedures that must be used to investigate crimes, arrest suspects, and carry out formal prosecution. The section of the Code of Criminal Procedure which discusses how an arrest is to be carried out, is an example of procedural law.[26]

THE DEFINITION AND CLASSIFICATION OF CRIME

In Michigan, a **crime** is defined as:

> an act or omission forbidden by law which is not designated as a civil infraction, and which is punishable upon conviction by any 1 or more of the following:
> (a) Imprisonment.
> (b) Fine not designated a civil fine.
> (c) Removal from office.
> (d) Disqualification to hold an office of trust, honor, or profit under the state.
> (e) Other penal discipline.[27]

There are two types of crimes in Michigan, **felonies** and **misdemeanors**.[28] A felony is defined in MCL §750.7 as "an offense for which the offender, on conviction may be punished by death, or by imprisonment in state prison." MCL §750.8 defines a misdemeanor as:

> When any act or omission, not a felony, is punishable according to law, by a fine, penalty or forfeiture, and imprisonment, or by such fine, penalty or forfeiture, or imprisonment, in the discretion of the court, such act or omission shall be deemed a misdemeanor.

In addition, according to MCL §750.9, if a statute prohibiting an action does not specify a penalty for violating the statute, the prohibited act is to be considered a misdemeanor.[29]

It is clear from this definition that, in many cases, the difference between a felony and a misdemeanor is not determined by the action committed by the offender but by the possible punishment prescribed in the Michigan Compiled Laws. Therefore, even if the statute does not specifically identify a crime as a misdemeanor or a felony, the classification can be inferred from the prescribed sentence.

The Criminal Act (*Actus Reus*) and Intent (*Mens Rea*)

In Michigan, for an individual to be considered criminally liable for his or her behavior, two key elements are necessary: ***actus reus*** (a criminal act) and ***mens rea*** (a guilty mind).

The first element, *actus reus*, involves a voluntary act committed by the offender. Most criminal acts are deliberate and voluntary. However, the act necessary to make up a crime will vary with each crime. Verbal actions (words) can be a sufficient action in, for example, the crime of perjury. Merely possessing something may be a sufficient act if the crime is one that involves illegal possession of goods (for example, possession of illegal drugs).

In some cases, a criminal act may also consist of an omission or failure to act. An **omission** occurs when someone who has a legal duty to act fails to perform an action that is required by law. For example, a security guard who deliberately looks the other way while company property is stolen is a passive participant and is guilty of an omission. Similarly, a parent or other legal caretaker who fails to adequately feed and shelter an infant, resulting in the death of the child, has committed a crime by his or her failure to act.

Failing to act is only a crime of omission when an individual has a legal duty to act in that situation. For example, consider the case of a swimmer at a local public pool who develops a cramp while in deep water. The lifeguard who is on duty at the pool has a legal duty to act and, if s/he fails to go to the swimmer's assistance, would be guilty of a crime of omission. However, the other swimmers in the pool have only a moral duty to aid the distressed swimmer and, if they fail to provide assistance, would not be guilty of any crime. In addition, the omission or failure to act must also be voluntary.

Mens rea involves the offender's mental state at the time of the criminal action. In addition to the voluntary criminal act, a **culpable mental state** may also be required. A culpable mental state means that the crime is committed intentionally, knowingly, recklessly, or with criminal negligence. A crime is committed **intentionally** when the offender consciously desires the outcome. Because intent is basically a state of mind, it may be inferred by the offender's actions. The offender does not have to declare intent to be convicted of a crime. A crime is committed **knowingly** when the offender is aware that s/he is engaging in conduct that violates the law. A crime is committed **recklessly** when the offender is aware of the risk created by his/her actions and consciously and unjustifiably disregards that risk. It may not always be necessary to prove the offender is personally aware of the risk, only that a reasonable person would consider the behavior as creating grave risk. Finally, **criminal negligence** occurs when the offender fails to recognize a risk that would be perceived by any reasonable person.

Strict liability offenses are crimes for which a culpable mental state, or *mens rea*, is not required. In these situations, the act alone, regardless of the offender's state of mind at the time of the act, is enough to create criminal liability. Strict liability crimes are fairly rare. One example of a strict liability crime is statutory rape, which involves intercourse with a person who is under the age of consent. A mistaken belief that the participant was not a minor is not a defense against such crimes in Michigan.

DEFENSES TO A CRIMINAL CHARGE

There are a wide variety of defenses to a criminal charge. Many of these are specifically mentioned in the Michigan Compiled Laws.

Justifications

A defendant who uses a **justification** defense admits to the commission of the criminal act but also claims that it was necessary to commit the act in order to avoid some greater evil or harm. Essentially, the defendant is not guilty of the crime s/he has been charged with because the reason for committing the act is one that the law considers to be a valid justification.

Probably the most well-known justification defense is that of **self-defense**, in which the defendant claims that the use of force against the victim was justifiable because it was the only way the defendant could ensure his/her own safety. Several statutes discuss the use of this defense as a defense for specific criminal acts. For example, MCL §750.234(b) states that it is a felony to intentionally discharge a firearm at a dwelling or occupied structure unless the individual does so in self-defense or to defend another. MCL §776.22(3)(b)(ii), which deals with how the police should handle domestic violence, states that a police officer should not make an arrest if "the officer has reasonable cause to believe the individual was acting in lawful self-defense or in lawful defense of another individual."

Another justification defense is that of **consent**. This defense claims that the victim voluntarily consented to the actions that caused the victimization. MCL §750.349 discusses the crime of kidnaping and states that:

> the consent thereto of the person, so taken, inveigled, kidnaped or confined, shall not be a defense, unless it shall be made satisfactorily to appear to the jury that such consent was not obtained by fraud nor extorted by duress or by threats.

In other words, a defendant charged with the crime of kidnaping cannot claim in his or her defense that the victim consented to the confinement unless s/he can show that the consent was voluntary. For example, in the case of *People v. Mackle*[30], a victim was kidnaped and sexually assaulted several times. Because the suspect told her that he would release her if she "behaved", she completed sexual acts with him under the belief that she was bargaining for her freedom. The court held that because the victim's release was conditional upon her performing a sexual act, her consent was coerced and was not voluntary.

Michigan is one of only twelve states that still retain the common law right to **resist an unlawful arrest**, another defense that falls into the category of justification. In the case of *City of Detroit v. Smith*[31], the courts stated that an individual is entitled to use reasonable force to resist an illegal arrest.

Excuses

A defendant using an **excuse** defense is claiming that at the time of the criminal act some circumstance or personal condition creates a situation under which s/he should not be held criminally accountable. The defendant is essentially claiming that s/he is not responsible, and should not be blamed for the act.

Probably the most well-known (and controversial) defense in this category is that of **insanity**. Although the term insanity is no longer used by mental health professionals, it is a legal term referring to a defense that is based on the defendant's claim that s/he was mentally ill or mentally incapacitated at the time of the offense. In Michigan, legal insanity is defined as:

> An individual is legally insane if, as a result of mental illness ... or as a result of being mentally retarded ... that person lacks substantial capacity either to appreciate the nature and quality or the wrongfulness of his or her conduct or to conform his or her conduct to the requirements of the law...[32]

It is clear from this definition that Michigan follows the **substantial capacity test** for insanity, as used in the Model Penal Code.

The burden of proof is on the defense to prove by a preponderance of the evidence that the defendant was insane at the time of the crime.[33] Defendants who intend to present a defense of insanity must provide advance notice to the prosecution. MCL §768.20a mandates pretrial notification of intent to rely on the insanity defense not less than 30 days before the trial date. The court will then order the defendant to undergo a psychiatric examination relating to the insanity claim. If the defendant fails to cooperate with this examination, s/he may be barred from presenting any testimony relating to his or her insanity at the trial. If the court finds that the defendant has a valid defense of insanity, s/he is found **not guilty by reason of insanity** and the court has the option of ordering the defendant to be committed for an indefinite period of time.[34] The state also allows for a verdict of **guilty but mentally ill**, which may be returned if the court finds that the defendant who is guilty of an offense was mentally ill but not legally insane at the time the crime was committed.[35] Mental illness is defined in MCL §330.2001a(5) as:

> a substantial disorder of thought or mood that significantly impairs judgment, behavior, capacity to recognize reality, or ability to cope with the ordinary demands of life.

Another defense that falls into the category of excuses is that of **intoxication**. In most cases, voluntary intoxication is not a defense to any crime proscribed by law. For example, MCL §768.21a(2) states that:

> An individual who was under the influence of voluntarily consumed or injected alcohol or controlled substances at the time of his or her alleged offense is not considered to have been legally insane solely because of being under the influence of the alcohol or controlled substances.

However, if the crime with which the defendant is charged is a specific intent crime, the level of intoxication may suffice to negate that element of the crime if the intoxication was sufficient to prevent the defendant from forming the necessary intent. This does not preclude the defendant from being convicted of a lesser included offense. For example, while the level of intoxication may negate the specific intent necessary to sustain a charge of first degree murder (which requires premeditation and deliberation), it does not necessarily prevent a conviction of second degree murder. Voluntary intoxication is not a defense for any crime that does not require specific intent.

In some cases, however, **involuntary intoxication** may serve as a complete defense if the defendant became intoxicated as the result of taking prescribed medication. To use this defense, the defendant must have had no way of knowing that the prescribed drug would have an intoxicating effect and must show that the intoxication rendered the defendant temporarily insane.[36]

The defense of **duress** or **coercion** generally requires that the defendant have committed the crime of which s/he is accused because the defendant has a reasonable fear that s/he or another person faces imminent death or serious bodily injury if s/he does not commit the act. One example would be a defendant who breaks and enters a home because s/he observes someone in the home requires immediate medical attention. The defense of duress may also involve the claim that the defendant's actions were committed under the control or influence of another person. An example of this type of duress would be a defendant who committed a robbery because his or her child was being held hostage and threatened. Duress may only be used when the crime that was committed prevents or avoids some greater harm. As a result, the defense of duress may not be used for the crime of homicide.[37]

Some states allow for a defense of **mistake of fact** or **ignorance of the law**. However, in Michigan, ignorance or mistake of law are not considered to be a defense to a criminal prosecution.[38]

Procedural Defenses

A **procedural defense** claims that some form of official procedure was not followed or that procedural law was not properly followed during the investigation or the prosecution of the crime. One procedural defense is the **denial of a speedy trial**. The right to a speedy trial is guaranteed by the Sixth Amendment to the United States Constitution and by Article I, Section 20 of the Michigan Constitution. In addition, MCL §768.1 states that:

The people of this state and persons charged with crime are entitled to and shall have a speedy trial and determination of all prosecutions and it is hereby made the duty of all public officers having duties to perform in any criminal case, to bring such case to a final determination without delay except as may be necessary to secure to the accused a fair and impartial trial.

The time limit for a trial to be "speedy" varies with the type of case (felony or misdemeanor), although the time limit may be extended under certain circumstances. For example, if the defendant requested or consented to an extension or delay of the trial date, s/he may not later claim that the right to a speedy trial was denied. MCR Rule 6.004 discusses the issue of a speedy trial and states that:

Whenever the defendant's constitutional right to a speedy trial is violated, the defendant is entitled to dismissal of the charge with prejudice.

Another issue is that of **double jeopardy**, which is discussed in the Fifth Amendment to the U.S. Constitution, and in Article I, Section 15 of the Michigan Constitution, which states that, "No person shall be subject for the same offense to be twice put in jeopardy." Protection against double jeopardy is also given in MCL §763.5.

Finally, the Michigan courts have stated that **entrapment** occurs:

if the police engaged in impermissible conduct which would induce a law-abiding person to commit a crime under similar circumstances, or the police engaged in conduct so reprehensible that it cannot be tolerated.[39]

Essentially the defense does not attempt to negate any element of the crime with which the defendant has been charged. Instead, the defense attempts to demonstrate that there are facts that justify barring the defendant from prosecution. The defendant must prove entrapment by a preponderance of the evidence.[40]

The entrapment defense, which is extremely difficult for the defendant to prove, is most commonly used when the defendant was ensnared in an undercover police action; the most frequent use seems to relate to the sale of illegal drugs. In general, the defendant will claim that s/he does not regularly sell drugs but made a sale as a favor to the undercover officer. One of the most common ways for the police to prevent the use of this defense is to make two or more purchases from the same suspect; after the suspect has made multiple sales, the jury is more likely to believe that the undercover officer simply provided the defendant with an opportunity to commit the crime, rather than that the officer induced or encouraged the defendant to engage in a behavior in which he/she would not normally become involved.

NOTES

1. The Michigan Constitution may be viewed online by going to the Official State of Michigan web site (http://www.michigan.gov/), selecting the "quick link" for the Michigan Legislature, and selecting the "Chapter Index" link under the heading "Michigan Compiled Laws Information". The Constitution is the first chapter of the Compiled Laws.
2. Michigan Constitution, Article XII, §1
3. Michigan Constitution, Article XII, §2
4. Michigan Constitution, Article XII, §3
5. Michigan Constitution, Article III, §2
6. Michigan Constitution, Article V, §21
7. Michigan Constitution, Article V, §30
8. Michigan Constitution, Article V, §3
9. Michigan Constitution, Article V, §22
10. Michigan Constitution, Article V, §14
11. Michigan Constitution, Article IV, §7
12. Michigan Constitution, Article IV, §8
13. Michigan Constitution, Article IV, §54
14. Michigan Constitution, Article V, §25
15. Michigan Constitution, Article VI, §2-3
16. Michigan Constitution, Article VI, §8-9
17. Michigan Constitution, Article VI, §11-12
18. Michigan Constitution, Article IV, §22
19. Michigan Constitution, Article IV, §26
20. "How does a Bill become a Law?"
   (http://www.michigan.gov/emi/0,1303,7-102-116-2836--,00.html)
21. *Ibid*
22. The Michigan Compiled Laws may be viewed online by going to the Official State of Michigan web site (http://www.michigan.gov/), selecting the "quick link" for the Michigan Legislature, and selecting the "Chapter Index" link under the heading "Michigan Compiled Laws Information".
23. MCL §780.651 - §780-659
24. MCL §780.751 - §780-911
25. MCR Rule 7.215(c)
26. MCL §764.1 *et.seq.*
27. MCL §750.5
28. MCL §750.6
29. Similar (but not identically worded) definitions of the terms "felony" and "misdemeanor" may be found in MCL §761.1(g) and (h) - Chapter I of the Michigan Code of Criminal Procedure.
30. *People v. Mackle*, 41 Mich App 583; 617 NW2d 339 (2000)
31. *City of Detroit v. Smith*, 235 Mich App 235; 597 NW2d 247 (1999)
32. MCL §768.21a(1); note that the statute includes specific definitions of mental illness and mental retardation which are not quoted here.

33.   MCL §768.21a(3)

34.   MCR Rule 6.304

35.   MCL §768.36(1)

36.   *People v. Caulley*, 197 Mich App 177; 494 NW2d 853 (1992), lv den 442 Mich 885; 502 NW2d 39 (1993)

37.   *People v Ramsdell*, 230 Mich App 386; 585 NW2d 1 (1998)

38.   *People v Munn*, 198 Mich App 726, 727; 499 NW2d 459 (1993)

39.   *People v Connolly*, 232 Mich App 425; 591 NW2d 340 (1998), lv den 460 Mich 867; 598 NW2d 341 (1999)

40.   *People v. Johnson*, 466 Mich 491 (2002)

CHAPTER 3

INDEX CRIMES

INTRODUCTION

The Federal Bureau of Investigation annually publishes the ***Uniform Crime Reports***[1] (UCR), the most widely used source of official data on crime and criminals in the United States. Much of the UCR deals with **index crimes**, a set of eight serious offenses that the FBI uses as a measure of crime in the United States. They are also known as **Part I Offenses** and include four violent crimes and four property crimes. The eight index crimes measured by the FBI are:

- homicide
- forcible rape
- robbery
- aggravated assault
- burglary
- larceny-theft
- motor-vehicle theft
- arson

However, the definitions used by the FBI in compiling the UCR are not always the same as those found in the Michigan Compiled Statutes. This chapter will discuss in detail these eight serious crimes as they are defined in Michigan.

CRIMINAL HOMICIDE

Homicide is the killing of one human being by another. If that killing is illegal, then it is a form of **criminal homicide**. The UCR includes the crimes of murder and nonnegligent manslaughter, which are defined as "the wilful (nonnegligent) killing of one human being by another."[2] In Michigan, homicide is discussed in Chapter XLV of the Michigan Penal Code and includes the crimes of:

- first degree murder
- second degree murder
- manslaughter
- negligent homicide

First Degree Murder

First degree murder is defined in MCL §750.316(1), which states that:

21

A person who commits any of the following is guilty of first degree murder and shall be punished by imprisonment for life:

(a) Murder perpetrated by means of poison, lying in wait, or any other willful, deliberate, and premeditated killing.
(b) Murder committed in the perpetration of, or attempt to perpetrate, arson, criminal sexual conduct in the first, second, or third degree, child abuse in the first degree, a major controlled substance offense, robbery, carjacking, breaking and entering of a dwelling, home invasion in the first or second degree, larceny of any kind, extortion, or kidnapping.
(c) A murder of a peace officer or a corrections officer committed while the peace officer or corrections officer is lawfully engaged in the performance of any of his or her duties as a peace officer or corrections officer, knowing that the peace officer or corrections officer is a peace officer or corrections officer engaged in the performance of his or her duty as a peace officer or corrections officer.

This statute identifies three specific categories of first degree murder: **premeditated murder**, **felony murder**, and **murder of specified law enforcement or corrections officers**. The first category involves the premeditated killing of another person, which basically refers to a killing in which the intent to kill was formed before the killing itself actually took place. According to the courts, premeditation and deliberation require that the offender had sufficient time to reconsider his or her actions.[3] The existence of premeditation and deliberation may be inferred from the circumstances of the crime.[4]

Felony murder, on the other hand, does not require premeditation on the part of the offender. It merely requires that the offender was engaged in one of the crimes listed in the statute and that death occurred while the offender was committing or attempting to commit that crime. If the death occurred while the offender was engaged in the commission of a crime that is not specifically listed in the statute, then the offender is not guilty of first degree felony murder, although the offender may still be guilty of some other type of homicide.

Finally, the third type of first degree murder has four elements. The first element is the commission of a murder, the second is that the victim was a peace or corrections officer, the third is that the victim was lawfully engaged in the performance of his/her duties at the time of the crime, and the fourth is that the offender knew the victim's identity as an officer and knew that s/he was performing lawful duties at the time of the murder. In this statute, Michigan is acknowledging the importance of providing protection to individuals who regularly risk their lives to serve and protect the public. The courts have held that classifying the killing of a peace or corrections officer as first degree murder, when the similar killing of a individual engaged in a different occupation might not be first degree murder, does not violate the equal protection clause of the constitution because it is related to a legitimate government interest, that of deterring the murder of public servants.[5]

Michigan does not have the death penalty. According to the statute, the mandatory sentence for the crime of first degree murder is life imprisonment.

Second Degree Murder

Second degree murder is discussed in MCL §750.317, which simply states that:

> All other kinds of murder shall be murder of the second degree, and shall be punished by imprisonment in the state prison for life, or any term of years, in the discretion of the court trying the same.

Essentially, second degree murder is any murder that does not fall under the definition of first degree murder in Michigan. According to the courts, second degree murder has four elements. These include:

1. A death must occur.
2. The death was caused by an act committed by the defendant.
3. The act was committed with malice.
4. The act was committed without justification.[6]

Malice has been defined as the intent to kill, cause great bodily harm, or commit an action with clear disregard of the likelihood that the action will cause death or great bodily harm. Based on this definition, the offender does not have to have specific intent to kill the victim for malicious intent to exist. The offender meets the conditions for malice if s/he intended to commit an inherently dangerous act.[7] For example, in the case of *People v. Abraham*[8], the defendant was shooting at trees with a rifle and injured two people (one fatally). Because the defendant had known that he might hit someone while shooting at the trees, he was found by the courts to have had malice and was convicted of second degree murder.

The statute specifies that second degree murder is punishable by imprisonment in a state prison for life or for some other period of time as determined by the trial court.

Manslaughter

MCL §750.312 states that:

> Any person who shall commit the crime of manslaughter shall be guilty of a felony punishable by imprisonment in the state prison, not more than 15 years or by fine of not more than 7,500 dollars, or both, at the discretion of the court.

The statute does not specifically define the crime of **manslaughter**; this is left to the courts. Michigan courts have recognized two types of manslaughter: voluntary and involuntary. **Voluntary manslaughter** involves the killing of another person without malice. Essentially, it involves a killing in the heat of passion, with provocation, and without any lapse of time in which a reasonable person might be expected to be able to control the passion that lead to the killing. Provocation is not an actual element of voluntary manslaughter but does serve to negate the presence of malice and distinguish the crime from second degree murder.[9]

Involuntary manslaughter is any unintentional unlawful killing that is not murder or voluntary manslaughter and does not involve malice or intent on the part of the offender.[10] This category covers four types of deaths. The first includes those cases not covered by the felony murder rule. In other words, involuntary manslaughter may be used in the case of a death that occurred during the commission of a crime that was not listed in MCL §750.316(1)(b). The second includes cases in which the death occurred as the result of an unlawful act that would not normally be expected to cause death or great bodily harm. An example of this type would be a death resulting from a minor assault because the victim was in some way especially vulnerable. The third category includes deaths resulting from a lawful act that was committed in a negligent manner. Finally, the fourth category includes deaths that result from the offender's negligent failure to prevent harm to the victim. However, for an offender to be charged with this crime, the offender must have a legal duty to the victim. For example, if an individual drowns in a swimming pool because the on-duty lifeguard failed to attempt a rescue, the lifeguard may be guilty of involuntary manslaughter because the lifeguard had a legal duty to the swimmers in the pool.

Negligent Homicide

Negligent homicide is a misdemeanor and is discussed in MCL §750.324, which states that:

> Any person who, by the operation of any vehicle upon any highway or upon any other property, public or private, at an immoderate rate of speed or in a careless, reckless or negligent manner, but not wilfully or wantonly, shall cause the death of another, shall be guilty of a misdemeanor, punishable by imprisonment in the state prison not more than 2 years or by a fine of not more than $2,000.00, or by both such fine and imprisonment.

Essentially, for an individual to be convicted of the crime of negligent homicide, the death must have involved the negligent use of a motor vehicle in some way. According to the courts, for a charge of criminal negligence as a result of an automobile accident to stand, the prosecution must show proof beyond a reasonable doubt that the defendant could have avoided the accident.[12]

According to MCL §750.325,

> The crime of negligent homicide shall be deemed to be included within every crime of manslaughter charged to have been committed in the operation of any vehicle, and in any case where a defendant is charged with manslaughter committed in the operation of any vehicle, if the jury shall find the defendant not guilty of the crime of manslaughter, it may render a verdict of guilty of negligent homicide.

The statute includes negligent homicide within the crime of manslaughter committed by operating a vehicle. As a result, a defendant may not be convicted of both crimes. According to the courts, both crimes (involuntary manslaughter and negligent homicide) address the same societal norm and both prohibit violations of this norm. Because the courts have concluded that the state legislature did not intend multiple punishments for the same conduct, convicting a defendant of both crimes for the death of a single victim violates the protection against double jeopardy.[12]

Non-Criminal Homicide

Although the UCR focuses specifically on criminal homicide, or murder, there are situations when the killing of one human being by another is lawful and therefore not a crime. Non-criminal homicides may be justifiable or excusable. An **excusable homicide** is a death that is caused by an accident or misfortune, when there is no unlawful intent involved in the act that caused the death. An automobile accident that does not involve negligence or any violation of the law on the part of the driver is an example of excusable homicide. A **justifiable homicide** is a killing that was committed by the use of justifiable deadly force, such as in self-defense.

There are no punishments associated with justifiable or excusable homicides as they are not forms of criminal homicide. If a homicide is ruled justifiable or excusable, the defendant at trial must be acquitted and released.

CRIMINAL SEXUAL CONDUCT

In the Uniform Crime Reporting Program, **forcible rape** is defined as "the carnal knowledge of a female forcibly and against her will."[13] In Michigan, Chapter LXXVI of the Michigan Penal Code is entitled "Rape", although the crime is actually known as **criminal sexual conduct** (CSC) in the statutes. Michigan recognizes four degrees of CSC.

First degree criminal sexual conduct is defined in MCL §750.520b(1), which states that:

> A person is guilty of criminal sexual conduct in the first degree if he or she engages in sexual penetration with another person and if any of the following circumstances exists:
> (a) That other person is under 13 years of age.
> (b) That other person is at least 13 but less than 16 years of age and any of the following:
>   1. The actor is a member of the same household as the victim.
>   2. The actor is related to the victim by blood or affinity to the fourth degree.
>   3. The actor is in a position of authority over the victim and used this authority to coerce the victim to submit.
>   4. The actor is a teacher, substitute teacher, or administrator of the public or nonpublic school in which that other person is enrolled.
> (c) Sexual penetration occurs under circumstances involving the commission of any other felony.
> (d) The actor is aided or abetted by 1 or more other persons and either of the following circumstances exists:

1. The actor knows or has reason to know that the victim is mentally incapable, mentally incapacitated, or physically helpless.
2. The actor uses force or coercion to accomplish the sexual penetration...

(e) The actor is armed with a weapon or any article used or fashioned in a manner to lead the victim to reasonably believe it to be a weapon.

(f) The actor causes personal injury to the victim and force or coercion is used to accomplish sexual penetration. Force or coercion includes but is not limited to any of the following circumstances:

1. When the actor overcomes the victim through the actual application of physical force or physical violence.
2. When the actor coerces the victim to submit by threatening to use force or violence on the victim, and the victim believes that the actor has the present ability to execute these threats.
3. When the actor coerces the victim to submit by threatening to retaliate in the future against the victim, or any other person, and the victim believes that the actor has the ability to execute this threat...
4. When the actor engages in the medical treatment or examination of the victim in a manner or for purposes which are medically recognized as unethical or unacceptable.
5. When the actor, through concealment or by the element of surprise, is able to overcome the victim.

(g) The actor causes personal injury to the victim, and the actor knows or has reason to know that the victim is mentally incapable, mentally incapacitated, or physically helpless.

(h) That other person is mentally incapable, mentally disabled, mentally incapacitated, or physically helpless, and any of the following:

1. The actor is related to the victim by blood or affinity to the fourth degree.
2. The actor is in a position of authority over the victim and used this authority to coerce the victim to submit.

Unlike the UCR definition, the Michigan statute is gender neutral. It does not specify the gender of the victim and specifically states that the offender may be either male or female. Therefore, in Michigan, either a male or female offender may be convicted of first degree CSC committed against either a male or female victim.

The statute does require some sexual penetration for the crime to occur. Sexual penetration has been defined as

> sexual intercourse, cunnilingus, fellatio, anal intercourse, or any other intrusion, however slight, of any part of a person's body or of any object into the genital or anal openings of another person's body, but emission of semen is not required.[14]

For the crime to be first degree CSC, sexual penetration must be combined with one of the conditions listed in the statute. Essentially, these conditions may be considered to be aggravating circumstances that increase the seriousness of the act to that of first degree CSC. The presence of any one of the listed circumstances is sufficient to sustain a charge of first degree CSC. For example, sexual penetration of a victim under the age of 13 is first degree CSC, regardless of the victim's relationship with the offender, the use of force or coercion, the presence of a weapon, or the existence of any other listed condition.

According to the statute, first degree CSC is a felony and is punishable by imprisonment in the state prison for life or for some term of years as determined by the court.

Second degree criminal sexual conduct is also a felony offense. It is defined in MCL §750.520c(1), which states that:

> A person is guilty of criminal sexual conduct in the second degree if the person engages in sexual contact with another person and if any of the following circumstances exists:
> (a) That other person is under 13 years of age.
> (b) That other person is at least 13 but less than 16 years of age and any of the following:
>   (i) The actor is a member of the same household as the victim.
>   (ii) The actor is related by blood or affinity to the fourth degree to the victim.
>   (iii) The actor is in a position of authority over the victim and the actor used this authority to coerce the victim to submit.
>   (iv) The actor is a teacher, substitute teacher, or administrator of the public or nonpublic school in which that other person is enrolled.
> (c) Sexual contact occurs under circumstances involving the commission of any other felony.
> (d) The actor is aided or abetted by 1 or more other persons and either of the following circumstances exists:
>   (i) The actor knows or has reason to know that the victim is mentally incapable, mentally incapacitated, or physically helpless.
>   (ii) The actor uses force or coercion to accomplish the sexual contact...
> (e) The actor is armed with a weapon, or any article used or fashioned in a manner to lead a person to reasonably believe it to be a weapon.
> (f) The actor causes personal injury to the victim and force or coercion is used to accomplish the sexual contact...
> (g) The actor causes personal injury to the victim and the actor knows or has reason to know that the victim is mentally incapable, mentally incapacitated, or physically helpless.
> (h) That other person is mentally incapable, mentally disabled, mentally incapacitated, or physically helpless, and any of the following:
>   (i) The actor is related to the victim by blood or affinity to the fourth degree.
>   (ii) The actor is in a position of authority over the victim and used this authority to coerce the victim to submit.
> (i) That other person is under the jurisdiction of the department of corrections and the actor is an employee or a contractual employee of, or a volunteer with, the department of corrections who knows that the other person is under the jurisdiction of the department of corrections.
> (j) That other person is under the jurisdiction of the department of corrections and the actor is an employee or a contractual employee of, or a volunteer with, a private vendor that

operates a youth correctional facility ... who knows that the other person is under the jurisdiction of the department of corrections.

(k) That other person is a prisoner or probationer under the jurisdiction of a county for purposes of imprisonment or a work program or other probationary program and the actor is an employee or a contractual employee of or a volunteer with the county or the department of corrections who knows that the other person is under the county's jurisdiction.

(l) The actor knows or has reason to know that a court has detained the victim in a facility while the victim is awaiting a trial or hearing, or committed the victim to a facility as a result of the victim having been found responsible for committing an act that would be a crime if committed by an adult, and the actor is an employee or contractual employee of, or a volunteer with, the facility in which the victim is detained or to which the victim was committed.

One key difference between first and second degree CSC is the basic behavior that must be committed for the crime to occur. Unlike first degree CSC, second degree CSC does not require sexual penetration but only sexual contact, which is defined as:

> the intentional touching of the victim's or actor's intimate parts or the intentional touching of the clothing covering the immediate area of the victim's or actor's intimate parts, if that intentional touching can reasonably be construed as being for the purpose of sexual arousal or gratification, done for a sexual purpose, or in a sexual manner for:
> (i)   Revenge.
> (ii)   To inflict humiliation.
> (iii) Out of anger.[15]

For the crime to be second degree CSC, sexual contact must be combined with one of the aggravating circumstances or conditions listed in the statute. The statute includes all of the conditions found in the statute defining first degree CSC as well as several others that apply when the offender is employed by a correctional agency and the victim is under the jurisdiction of that agency. As with the more serious crime, the presence of any one of the circumstances listed in the statute is sufficient to sustain a charge of second degree CSC.

Second degree CSC is punishable by imprisonment for up to fifteen years.[16]

Third degree criminal sexual conduct is defined in MCL §750.520(d)(1), which states that:

> A person is guilty of criminal sexual conduct in the third degree if the person engages in sexual penetration with another person and if any of the following circumstances exist:
> (a)   That other person is at least 13 years of age and under 16 years of age.
> (b)   Force or coercion is used to accomplish the sexual penetration...
> (c)   The actor knows or has reason to know that the victim is mentally incapable, mentally incapacitated, or physically helpless.

28

(d) That other person is related to the actor by blood or affinity to the third degree and the sexual penetration occurs under circumstances not otherwise prohibited by this chapter...This subdivision does not apply if both persons arc lawfully married to each other at the time of the alleged violation.

(e) That other person is at least 16 years of age but less than 18 years of age and a student at a public or nonpublic school, and the actor is a teacher, substitute teacher, or administrator of that public or nonpublic school. This subdivision does not apply if the other person is emancipated or if both persons are lawfully married to each other at the time of the alleged violation.

As with first degree CSC, the crime prohibits sexual penetration of another person under circumstances enumerated in the statute. The circumstances listed in this statute are similar to, but not considered to be as serious as, those found in the first degree CSC statute. For example, an offender is guilty of *third degree CSC* if s/he engages in sexual penetration with a victim who is at least 13 years old but less than 16 years old. The charge would be increased to first-degree CSC if the offender and victim were related by blood or affinity to the fourth degree.

Third degree CSC is punishable by imprisonment for not more than fifteen years.[17]

Finally, **fourth degree criminal sexual conduct** parallels second degree CSC by involving sexual contact rather than penetration. It is defined as:

A person is guilty of criminal sexual conduct in the fourth degree if he or she engages in sexual contact with another person and if any of the following circumstances exist:

(a) That other person is at least 13 years of age but less than 16 years of age, and the actor is 5 or more years older than that other person.

(b) Force or coercion is used to accomplish the sexual contact. Force or coercion includes, but is not limited to, any of the following circumstances:

(i) When the actor overcomes the victim through the actual application of physical force or physical violence.

(ii) When the actor coerces the victim to submit by threatening to use force or violence on the victim, and the victim believes that the actor has the present ability to execute that threat.

(iii) When the actor coerces the victim to submit by threatening to retaliate in the future against the victim, or any other person, and the victim believes that the actor has the ability to execute that threat...

(iv) When the actor engages in the medical treatment or examination of the victim in a manner or for purposes which are medically recognized as unethical or unacceptable.

(v) When the actor achieves the sexual contact through concealment or by the element of surprise.

(c) The actor knows or has reason to know that the victim is mentally incapable, mentally incapacitated, or physically helpless.

(d) That other person is related to the actor by blood or affinity to the third degree and the sexual contact occurs under circumstances not otherwise prohibited by this chapter ... This subdivision does not apply if both persons are lawfully married to each other at the time of the alleged violation.

(e) The actor is a mental health professional and the sexual contact occurs during or within 2 years after the period in which the victim is his or her client or patient and not his or her spouse...

(f) That other person is at least 16 years of age but less than 18 years of age and a student at a public or nonpublic school, and the actor is a teacher, substitute teacher, or administrator of that public or nonpublic school. This subdivision does not apply if the other person is emancipated or if both persons are lawfully married to each other at the time of the alleged violation.

As with second degree CSC, the crime prohibits sexual contact with another person under circumstances enumerated in the statute. The circumstances listed in this statute are similar to, but not considered to be as serious as, those found in the second degree CSC statute. For example, an offender is guilty of fourth degree CSC if s/he engages in sexual penetration with a victim who is at least 13 years old but less than 16 years old only if the offender is at least five years older than the victim. The charge would be increased to second degree CSC if the offender and victim were related by blood or affinity to the fourth degree, regardless of the age difference between the two.

Fourth degree CSC is a misdemeanor and is punishable by imprisonment for up to two years, or by a fine of up to $500, or by both penalties.

Unlike some states, Michigan does not recognize the crime of **statutory rape** as a specific crime but includes it in the CSC statutes. Statutory rape is generally considered to involve non-forcible sexual activities with a minor. All four degrees of CSC in Michigan prohibit sexual contact with victims under the age of 16.

Michigan has eliminated the marital exemption for most types of CSC. MCL §750.520l specifically states that:

A person may be charged and convicted under sections 520b to 520g even though the victim is his or her legal spouse. However, a person may not be charged or convicted solely because his or her legal spouse is under the age of 16, mentally incapable, or mentally incapacitated.

However, there are certain exceptions to this. For example, the definition of fourth degree statutory rape includes a condition that criminalizes sexual contact between a mental health professional and his or her client or patient during, and for two years after, the period of treatment. However, the statute specifically states that this condition does not apply when the two individuals are married.

ROBBERY

The FBI's Uniform Crime Reporting Program defines **robbery** as "the taking or attempting to take anything of value from the care, custody, or control of a person or persons by force or threat of force or violence and/or by putting the victim in fear."[18] In Michigan, robbery is discussed in Chapter LXXVIII of the *Michigan Penal Code*. The courts have stated that "A robbery is a larceny aggravated by the use of force or threat of force to accomplish the taking from a person or in his presence."[19]

The state recognizes four types of robbery:

- armed robbery
- carjacking
- unarmed robbery
- bank, safe, and vault robbery.

Although all types of robbery contain elements of theft, because the crime includes violence against the victim and threatens the victim's safety and security, robbery is considered to be an offense against the person, rather than a property crime. The taking of property is considered to be secondary to the use of violence or force against the victim.[20]

The statute defining **armed robbery** states that:

> Any person who shall assault another, and shall feloniously rob, steal and take from his person, or in his presence, any money or other property, which may be the subject of larceny, such robber being armed with a dangerous weapon, or any article used or fashioned in a manner to lead the person so assaulted to reasonably believe it to be a dangerous weapon, shall be guilty of a felony, punishable by imprisonment in the state prison for life or for any term of years. If an aggravated assault or serious injury is inflicted by any person while committing an armed robbery as defined in this section, the sentence shall be not less than 2 years' imprisonment in the state prison.[21]

Essentially, the crime has three elements:

1. The offender commits an assault.
2. The offender feloniously takes property from the person or presence of the victim.
3. The offender is armed with a dangerous weapon or some object that the victim reasonably believes to be a dangerous weapon.

For the crime of robbery to occur, the courts have held that the assault against the victim must occur prior to, or at the same time as, the taking of the property. If force is used after the property has been taken, as a way of retaining the stolen property rather than as a way of actually taking it, the required element of force or violence to accomplish the larceny has not been established.[22]

31

The courts have also discussed the issue of what constitutes a "dangerous weapon." They have determined that it rests not only on what the object is but also how it was used during the criminal event. Essentially, the term includes any object that has been designed to be dangerous and is capable of causing death or serious injury to the victim (e.g., a firearm). It may also include any object that is capable of causing death or serious injury that was used by the offender as a weapon. For example, in the case of *People v. Norris*, the court held that tear gas could be considered a dangerous weapon.[23] Actual possession of a weapon by the offender is required by the statute. Using words or threats to obtain property from the victim is not sufficient to prove a charge of robbery without some objective evidence of the existence of a weapon.[24]

Unarmed robbery is defined in MCL §750.530, which states that:

> Any person who shall, by force and violence, or by assault or putting in fear, feloniously rob, steal and take from the person of another, or in his presence, any money or other property which may be the subject of larceny, such robber not being armed with a dangerous weapon, shall be guilty of a felony, punishable by imprisonment in the state prison not more than 15 years.

The three elements of an unarmed robbery are:

1. The offender uses force, violence, or assault, or puts the victim in fear
2. The offender feloniously takes property from the person or presence of the victim
3. The offender is not armed with a dangerous weapon

The only difference between the two crimes is the presence or absence of a dangerous weapon. It is clear that the crime is considered somewhat less serious because the unarmed robbery statute sets a maximum limit of 15 years on the length of the sentence that may be imposed, while the armed robbery statute permits a sentence of life imprisonment.

Recently, Michigan codified the crime of **carjacking,** which is a form of robbery. MCL §750.529a states that:

> (1) A person who by force or violence, or by threat of force or violence, or by putting in fear robs, steals, or takes a motor vehicle ... from another person, in the presence of that person or the presence of a passenger or in the presence of any other person in lawful possession of the motor vehicle, is guilty of carjacking, a felony punishable by imprisonment for life or for any term of years.
>
> (2) A sentence imposed for a violation of this section may be imposed to run consecutively to any other sentence imposed for a conviction that arises out of the same transaction.

The crime of carjacking has three elements:

1. The offender takes a motor vehicle from another person.
2. The taking was committed in the presence of someone in lawful possession of the motor vehicle (including a passenger).
3. The taking was accomplished by the use or threat of force or violence, or by putting the victim in fear.

The victim does not need to be the owner of the vehicle, only to have custody of the vehicle at the time of the crime. The crime does not require that the offender intend to permanently deprive the victim of the vehicle, only that s/he intended to commit the acts of force, threats or fear to take the motor vehicle from the victim in his/her presence.

Although carjacking is a form of robbery, the carjacking and robbery statutes have different purposes. The purpose of the carjacking statute is to prohibit the taking of a motor vehicle by force or threat of force. The purpose of the armed robbery statute is to prohibit the taking of property by assault and the use of a dangerous weapon. Because of this, the courts have held that an offender may be convicted of and punished for both crimes without a violation of the state's protections against double jeopardy.[25]

Finally, Michigan specifically recognizes the crime of **bank, safe, and vault robbery**. The crime is defined as:

> Any person who, with intent to commit the crime of larceny, or any felony, shall confine, maim, injure or wound, or attempt, or threaten to confine, kill, maim, injure or wound, or shall put in fear any person for the purpose of stealing from any building, bank, safe or other depository of money, bond or other valuables, or shall by intimidation, fear or threats compel, or attempt to compel any person to disclose or surrender the means of opening any building, bank, safe, vault or other depository of money, bonds, or other valuables, or shall attempt to break, burn, blow up or otherwise injure or destroy any safe, vault or other depository of money, bonds or other valuables in any building or place, shall, whether he succeeds or fails in the perpetration of such larceny or felony, be guilty of a felony, punishable by imprisonment in the state prison for life or any term of years.[26]

ASSAULT AND BATTERY

There is often some confusion about the actual meaning of **assault**. In some states (e.g., Florida, California, Illinois), assault does not actually involve the infliction of an injury upon another person; it is merely an intentional attempt or threat to cause an injury. In these states, when an injury is actually inflicted, a **battery** has occurred. The Michigan statutes are rather inconsistent. The statutes frequently use the terms "assault" and "assault and battery" interchangeably, so that the term "assault" may be used in reference to an act that requires striking a victim. Therefore, the term "assault" will be used in this section to include "battery" as well.

The Uniform Crime Reporting Program also considers assault to involve the actual injury of another person. The UCR focuses specifically on aggravated assault, which it defines as:

> an unlawful attack by one person upon another for the purpose of inflicting severe or aggravated bodily injury. This type of assault is usually accompanied by the use of a weapon or by means likely to produce death or great bodily harm.[27]

In Michigan, **simple assault** is defined by the common law, rather than by statute. It essentially consists of "an attempt to commit a battery or an unlawful act which places another in reasonable apprehension of receiving an immediate battery."[28]

Felonious assault is defined in MCL §750.82, and consists of:

> a person who assaults another person with a gun, revolver, pistol, knife, iron bar, club, brass knuckles, or other dangerous weapon without intending to commit murder or to inflict great bodily harm less than murder is guilty of a felony ...

Essentially, felonious assault is a simple assault that is aggravated by the use of a weapon. Felonious assault is punishable by imprisonment for not more than four years, a fine of up to $2,000, or both the term of imprisonment and the fine. However, if the crime is committed in a weapon-free school zone, the offender may be punished by a term of imprisonment for up to four years, a fine of up to $6,000, a sentence of up to 150 hours of community service, or any combination of these.[29]

The definition of felonious assault includes the requirement that the offender did not intend to murder the victim, or to cause great bodily harm to the victim. If an offender commits an assault with the intent of murdering the victim, the crime is considered to be **assault with intent to commit murder** and is punishable by imprisonment for life or some other term of years.[30] This is different from the crime of attempted murder, which is defined in MCL §750.91 and which includes murder attempts that do not involve an assault. Similarly, if the offender commits an assault with the intent of causing great bodily harm, the offense is defined in MCL §750.84 as **assault with intent to do great bodily harm less than murder**. It is not necessary for any physical injury to be caused for an offender to be charged with this crime. Threats and actions may be sufficient to prove intent.[31]

The Michigan Compiled Laws specific a number of other types of assault with intent. These include:

- assault with intent to maim[32]
- assault with intent to commit felony not otherwise punished[33]
- assault with intent to rob and steal, unarmed[34]
- assault with intent to rob and steal, armed[35]

These are all felony crimes punishable by some term of imprisonment in the state prison as specified in the individual statutes.

BURGLARY

The UCR defines **burglary** as the "unlawful entry of a structure to commit a felony or theft."[36] However, Michigan does not have a general offense entitled "burglary". Generic burglary offenses are classified under various forms and levels of **breaking and entering**, and are discussed in Chapter XVI of the Michigan Penal Code. The crime that best corresponds to burglary as defined by the UCR is outlined in MCL §750.110, which states that:

> A person who breaks and enters, with intent to commit a felony or a larceny therein, a tent, hotel, office, store, shop, warehouse, barn, granary, factory or other building, structure, boat, ship, or railroad car is guilty of a felony, punishable by imprisonment for not more than 10 years.

Essentially, this crime has three elements:

1. The offender breaks into a building.
2. The offender enters the building.
3. The offender intended to commit a felony or larceny in the building at the time of the breaking and entering.

The element of breaking requires that the offender did not have the legal right to enter the building and that the offender used some amount of force to open a door or window and create an entrance to the building. Essentially, breaking involves creating an opening in the building. The courts have held that opening a closed but unlocked door is sufficient to constitute breaking.[37] However, if the door or window is already opened, the element of breaking has not been met. An offender who has a legal right to enter a building may still meet the element of breaking by breaking into an inner area of the building where s/he does not have legal access. For example, an offender may have the right to enter a department store but does not have the legal right to enter a room marked "Staff Only - Keep Out." Opening the door to this room would be sufficient to constitute breaking under the law. The court must also prove that the offender, when breaking and entering the building, had the intent to commit a felony or larceny. If the offender cannot be shown to have intent, s/he may not be found guilty of felony breaking and entering with intent. However, s/he may be found guilty of the misdemeanor crime of breaking and entering without permission.[38]

The crime only requires that the offender intended to commit a larceny or felony. It is not necessary for the prosecution to prove that the defendant actually committed or even attempted to commit the crime to convict. However, if there is no such intent, or if the intent was not formed until after the offender has gained entry to the dwelling, the element of intent has not been met. For example, if a defendant can prove that s/he committed the breaking and entering of a building for a non-criminal purpose (e.g., to obtain shelter from a storm), the defendant may not be convicted of the crime of breaking and entering with intent to commit a larceny or felony. Even if the defendant eventually did commit a larceny or felony on the premises, the element is not met because there was no criminal intent prior to entering the building.

All three elements must be proved separately for an offender to be convicted of felony breaking and entering. The courts have held that the element of unlawful entry is separate from the element of intent, so that a wrongful intent does not negate the need for an unlawful entry, or make it illegal to enter a building when one has the right to do so. In the case of *People v. Cornell*, several individuals agreed to steal guns from the home of one offender's stepfather. The offender lived in the home, had permission to enter the home freely, and had permission to bring friends into the house. Because of this, the entry into the house was not illegal, despite the offenders' intent to steal after entering the house.[39]

If the building in question is a dwelling, the crime is known as **home invasion** and is considered to be a more serious offense. There are three levels or degrees of felony home invasion as defined in the statutes. MCL §750.110a(2) states that:

> A person who breaks and enters a dwelling with intent to commit a felony, larceny, or assault in the dwelling, a person who enters a dwelling without permission with intent to commit a felony, larceny, or assault in the dwelling, or a person who breaks and enters a dwelling or enters a dwelling without permission and, at any time while he or she is entering, present in, or exiting the dwelling, commits a felony, larceny, or assault is guilty of home invasion in the first degree if at any time while the person is entering, present in, or exiting the dwelling either of the following circumstances exists:
> (a) The person is armed with a dangerous weapon.
> (b) Another person is lawfully present in the dwelling.

First degree home invasion is punishable by imprisonment for up to 20 years, or by a fine of up to $5,000, or by both the fine and the prison term.[40]

Second degree home invasion is defined in MCL §750.110a(3) and differs from first degree home invasion in that the aggravating circumstances listed in the first statute (the offender is armed with a dangerous weapon or the lawful presence of another person in the dwelling) are not required for this crime. Second degree home invasion is punishable by imprisonment for up to 15 years and/or a fine of up to $3,000.[41]

Third degree home invasion is defined in MCL §750.110a(4), which states that:

> A person is guilty of home invasion in the third degree if the person does either of the following
> (a) Breaks and enters a dwelling with intent to commit a misdemeanor in the dwelling, enters a dwelling without permission with intent to commit a misdemeanor in the dwelling, or breaks and enters a dwelling or enters a dwelling without permission and, at any time while he or she is entering, present in, or exiting the dwelling, commits a misdemeanor.
> (b) Breaks and enters a dwelling or enters a dwelling without permission and, at any time while the person is entering, present in, or exiting the

36

dwelling, violates any of the following ordered to protect a named person or persons:

(i)   A probation term or condition.
(ii)   A parole term or condition.
(iii) A personal protection order term or condition.
(iv)   A bond or bail condition or any condition of pretrial release.

Although in this statute the offender only has intent to commit, or actually does commit, a misdemeanor offense, the elements of breaking and entering raise the seriousness of this offense to a felony. Third degree home invasion is punishable by imprisonment for up to five years and/or a fine of up to $2,000.[42]

To be found guilty of any degree of home invasion, the building in question must be a dwelling. MCL §750.110a(a) specifically defines a dwelling as, "a structure or shelter that is used permanently or temporarily as a place of abode, including an appurtenant structure attached to that structure or shelter."

Finally, MCL §750.112 specifically discusses the crime of **burglary with explosives**. This is one of a very few times that the term "burglary" is actually used in the Michigan Consolidated Laws.[43] The statute states that:

> Any person who enters any building, and for the purpose of committing any crime therein, uses or attempts to use nitro-glycerine, dynamite, gunpowder or any other high explosive, shall be guilty of a felony, punishable by imprisonment in the state prison not less than 15 years nor more than 30 years.

Essentially, this crime requires the entry of a building (not just a dwelling) as well as the intent to commit a crime within the building. In addition, the crime requires that the offender uses or attempts to use one of the explosives listed in the statute. Intent to use explosives is not sufficient to satisfy this element of the crime; the offender must actually use or attempt to use the explosive device to be convicted of this crime.

LARCENY-THEFT

The FBI defines **larceny-theft** as:

> the unlawful taking, carrying, leading, or riding away of property from the possession or constructive possession of another. It includes crimes such as shoplifting, pocket-picking, purse-snatching, thefts from motor vehicles, thefts of motor vehicle parts and accessories, bicycle thefts, etc., in which no use of force, violence, or fraud occurs.[44]

In Michigan, the equivalent crime is known as **larceny** and is discussed in Chapter LII of the Michigan Penal Code. According to MCL §750.356(1),

> A person who commits larceny by stealing any of the following property of another person is guilty of a crime as provided in this section:
> (a)   Money, goods, or chattels.
> (b)   A bank note, bank bill, bond, promissory note, due bill, bill of exchange or other bill, draft, order, or certificate.
> (c)   A book of accounts for or concerning money or goods due, to become due, or to be delivered.
> (d)   A deed or writing containing a conveyance of land or other valuable contract in force.
> (e)   A receipt, release, or defeasance.
> (f)   A writ, process, or public record.

According to the courts, larceny has five essential elements:

1. Taking goods or property
2. Carrying away (asportation)
3. Felonious intent
4. The items taken must be the goods or property of another person
5. The items were taken without the consent and against the will of the owner.[45]

The victim does not have to be the owner of the property. S/he only has to have legal possession of the property at the time of the crime. Essentially, the "owner" is the individual who, at the time of the larceny, had rightful possession and control of the property. However, the offender must know that s/he is not entitled to the property. Thus, if the offender honestly believed that s/he owned the property and had a right to possess and control it, regardless of the truth of this belief, the offender is not guilty of the crime of larceny.[46]

The seriousness of the crime and the associated punishment depends on the value of the property stolen and the offender's prior record:

- If the value of the stolen property is at least $20,000, or if the value is between $10,000 and $20,000 and the offender has at least two prior convictions for this crime, the crime is a felony and is punishable either by imprisonment for up to 10 years, or by a fine of up to $15,000 or three times the value of the stolen property (whichever is greater), or by both the fine and the term of incarceration.[47]

- If the value of the property stolen is between $10,000 and $20,000, or if the value is between $200 and $10,000 and the offender has at least one prior conviction for this crime, the crime is a felony and punishment for the offense is imprisonment for up to five years and/or a fine of up to $10,000 or three times the value of the stolen property (whichever is greater).[48]

- If the property is worth between $200 and $10,000 or if the property is valued at less than $200 and the offender has at least one prior conviction, the crime is a misdemeanor punishable by imprisonment for up to one year and/or a fine of up to $2,000 or three times the value of the stolen property (whichever is greater).[49]

- If the property is valued at less than $200, the crime is a misdemeanor punishable by no more than 93 days and/or a fine of up to $500 or three times the value of the stolen property (whichever is greater).[50]

If the property is stolen directly from the victim's person, the crime is known as **larceny from the person**. This crime is considered to be more serious than basic larceny, and is a felony punishable by imprisonment for up to ten years, regardless of the value of the property stolen.[51] The difference between this crime and that of robbery is the element of force. If the offender uses force, violence, or assault, or puts the victim in fear, the crime is that of robbery. If the offender uses a dangerous weapon, the crime is that of armed robbery.

Some of the other categories of larceny that are specifically defined by statute in Michigan include:

- larceny from a motor vehicle or trailer[52]
- larceny of livestock[53]
- stealing firearms of another[54]
- larceny at a fire[55]
- larceny from a vacant building or dwelling[56]
- larceny from libraries[57]
- larceny from car or persons detained or injured by accident[58]

MOTOR VEHICLE THEFT

The UCR considers **motor vehicle theft** to be a separate index crime from that of theft or larceny-theft. It is defined by the FBI as:

the theft or attempted theft of a motor vehicle, this offense category includes the stealing of automobiles, trucks, buses, motorcycles, motorscooters, snowmobiles, etc.[59]

In Michigan, the theft of a motor vehicle generally falls under the crime of larceny. However, there are several other crimes which also correspond to this index crime. Chapter LXI of the Michigan Penal Code, which discusses crimes relating to motor vehicles, includes the crime of **taking possession of and driving away a motor vehicle**. According to MCL §750.413,

> Any person who shall, wilfully and without authority, take possession of and drive or take away, and any person who shall assist in or be a party to such taking possession, driving or taking away of any motor vehicle, belonging to another, shall be guilty of a felony, punishable by imprisonment in the state prison for not more than 5 years.

To sustain this crime, the offender must both take and operate the vehicle. Thus, if the offender took the vehicle legally but operated it unlawfully (e.g., the offender did not have a license to operate the vehicle), s/he could not be convicted of this crime.

MCL §750.362a(1) defines the crime of **larceny of a rented motor vehicle** as:

> A person to whom a motor vehicle, trailer, or other tangible property is delivered on a rental or lease basis under a written agreement providing for its return to a particular place at a particular time who with intent to defraud the lessor refuses or willfully neglects to return the vehicle, trailer, or other tangible property after expiration of the time stated in a written notice mailed by registered or certified mail addressed to that person's last known address is guilty of larceny, punishable as provided in this section.

The level of this crime (felony or misdemeanor) and the actual punishment depend on the value of the property stolen and the prior criminal record of the offender.

In addition, carjacking is defined in MCL §750.529a (see the discussion under **Robbery** earlier in this chapter) and does involve the taking of a motor vehicle from another's person or custody. In Michigan, carjacking is considered to be a form of robbery rather than a theft.

ARSON

Like burglary, the common-law felony crime of **arson** was a crime against a home or dwelling place. While it could occur at any time of day, nighttime arson was considered to be a more serious crime. The UCR defines arson as:

> any willful or malicious burning or attempt to burn, with or without intent to defraud, a dwelling house, public building, motor vehicle or aircraft, personal property of another, etc.[60]

In Michigan, the crime of burning property is not statutorily defined as arson, but as **burning**. The term "burn" is defined as:

> setting fire to, or doing any act which results in the starting of a fire, or aiding, counseling, inducing, persuading or procuring another to do such act or acts.[61]

The Michigan statutes include different categories of burning, based on the type of property targeted by the offender: real property, personal property, or a dwelling. MCL §750.72 defines the crime of **burning of a dwelling house**:

> Any person who wilfully or maliciously burns any dwelling house, either occupied or unoccupied, or the contents thereof, whether owned by himself or another, or any building within the curtilage of such dwelling house, or the contents thereof, shall be guilty of a felony, punishable by imprisonment in the state prison not more than 20 years.

This is considered to be the most serious type of burning, because of the increased likelihood of injury to a person.

The requirement that the crime be committed willfully or maliciously means that the offender intended to burn the dwelling, or that the defendant committed an act that reasonably would result in the burning of the dwelling, and that the act was voluntary and unjustified. The dwelling must be burned but does not have to be totally destroyed. Damage to some part of the structure is sufficient.

If the real property targeted is not a dwelling, the crime is known as **burning of other real property**. According to MCL §750.73,

> Any person who wilfully or maliciously burns any building or other real property, or the contents thereof, other than those specified in the next preceding section of this chapter, the property of himself or another, shall be guilty of a felony, punishable by imprisonment in the state prison for not more than 10 years.

While this crime is a felony, it is clear from the maximum term of imprisonment specified in the statute that it is not considered to be as serious an offense as the burning of a dwelling.

The crime of **burning of personal property** involves the willful and malicious burning of any personal property (other than real property or a dwelling), that is owned by the offender or another person. The seriousness of this crime (felony or misdemeanor) and the associated punishment depend on the value of the property burned and the offender's prior record.[62]

In addition, any burning of insured personal or real property, with intent to defraud the insurance company, is a felony offense punishable by up to ten years incarceration in the state prison.[63] According to the courts, it is possible to convict an offender of both the crime of burning of a dwelling and burning of insured property without violation of the state's protections against double jeopardy because the statutes have different purposes and different elements, and protect different people.[64]

The courts have also held that each time a building is burned, an offense of burning is committed, regardless of the number of individual fires that were set. Therefore, an offender may be convicted of multiple counts if several buildings were burned, even though only a single fire was set.[65]

Despite the fact that no statute in the Michigan Penal Code defines the crime of "arson", the definition of first degree felony murder includes arson as one of the underlying felonies.[66] The courts have stated that in this situation, the common law definition of arson applies when charging an offender with felony murder by arson. The common law meaning of arson was limited to the intentional burning of a dwelling place. Therefore, the crime of felony murder by arson can only occur if death occurred as the result of the burning of a dwelling. In the case of *People v. Reeves*, the offenders set fire to an uninhabitable building. The building collapsed, killing a firefighter. Because the targeted building was uninhabitable, the offenders could not be charged with first degree felony murder.[67]

HATE CRIMES

Hate or bias crimes are not specifically included among the UCR's eight index crimes. However, the FBI began to collect data on this category of crime after President Bush signed the Hate Crimes Statistics Act in 1990. The UCR defines hate or bias crimes as "those offenses motivated in part or singularly by personal prejudice against others because of a diversity—race, sexual orientation, religion, ethnicity/national origin, or disability.[68]

In Michigan, the chief of each police department and the sheriff of each county is required to report to the state police information on bias or hate crimes.[69] According to the Michigan State Police, a hate/bias crime is defined as:

> a criminal offense committed against a person or property which is motivated, in whole or in part, by the offender's bias against a race, religion, ethnic/national origin, sexual orientation or disability group.[70]

According to Michigan State Police Department's 2001 statistics on crime in Michigan, 569 hate/bias crime offenses were reported, affecting a total of 625 victims. These crimes included crimes against persons, such as murder, robbery, and aggravated assault, and property crimes such as burglary, larceny, and arson. The most common violent hate crimes were intimidation/stalking (31 percent) and simple or non-aggravated assault (22 percent). The most common property hate crime was vandalism (16 percent).[71]

The most frequent motivation was the race or color of the victim; approximately 55 percent of the 569 reported hate crimes were motivated by the victim's race or color (anti-black and anti-white motivations predominated). Other motivations included the victim's sexual orientation (12 percent - this included not only anti-homosexual but also anti-bisexual and anti-heterosexual offenses), religion (11 percent), ethnicity or national origin (11 percent), gender (8 percent), and disability (2 percent).[72]

Like other states, Michigan has experienced a recent increase in anti-Islamic (Moslem) hate crimes. During the four-year period between 1997 and 2000, there were a total of 32 hate crimes motived by anti-Islamic religious bias. During 2001, there were a total of 42 such crimes. This increase may be due at least in part to the terrorist attacks of September 11, 2001.[73]

NOTES

1.   Recent issues of the *Uniform Crime Reports* may be viewed online on the Federal Bureau of Investigation's website (http://www.fbi.gov/ucr/ucr.htm)
2.   *Uniform Crime Reports* (http://www.fbi.gov/ucr/ucr.htm)
3.   *People v. Graves*, 224 Mich App 676; 569 NW2d 911 (1997), mod 458 Mich 476; 581 NW2d 299 (1998), lv den after rem 461 Mich 883; 603 NW2d 779 (1999)
4.   *Ibid*
5.   *People v. Clark*, 243 Mich App 424; 622 NW2d 344 (2001)
6.   *People v Goecke*, 457 Mich 442; 579 NW2d 868 (1998)
7.   *Ibid*
8.   *People v. Abraham*, 256 Mich App 265 (2003)
9.   *People v. Mendoza* 468 Mich 527 (2003)
10.   *Ibid*
11.   *People v. Timms*, 449 Mich 83; 534 NW2d 675 (1995), reh den 450 NW2d 1204; 539 NW2d 375 (1995)
12.   *People v. Herron*, 464 Mich 593 (2001)
13.   *Uniform Crime Reports, op. cit.*
14.   MCL §750.521a(m)
15.   MCL §750.521a(l)
16.   MCL §750.520(c)(2)
17.   MCL §750.520(d)(2)
18.   *Uniform Crime Reports, op cit.*
19.   *People v. Randolph*, 466 Mich 532 (2002)
20.   *People v. Hendricks*, 446 Mich 435; 521 NW2d 546 (1994), reh den 447 Mich 1202; 525 NW2d 453 (1994)
21.   MCL §750.529
22.   *People v. Scruggs*, 256 Mich App 303 (2003); see also *People v. Randolph, op. cit.*
23.   *People v. Norris*, 236 Mich App 411; 600 NW2d 658 (1999)
24.   *People v. Jolly*, 442 Mich 458; 502 NW2d 177 (1993)
25.   *People v. Parker*, 230 Mich App 337; 584 NW2d 336 (1998), lv den 459 Mich 987; 593 NW2d 557 (1999)

26. MCL §750.531

27. *Uniform Crime Reports, op cit.*

28. *People v. Grant*, 211 Mich App 200; 535 NW2d 581 (1995)

29. MCL §750.82(2)

30. MCL §750.83

31. *People v. Harrington*, 227 Mich App 236; 575 NW2d 316 (1997), lv den 459 Mich 971; 591 NW2d 40 (1999)

32. MCL §750.86

33. MCL §750.87

34. MCL §750.88

35. MCL §750.89

36. *Uniform Crime Reports, op cit.*

37. *People v. Toole*, 227 Mich App 656; 576 NW2d 441 (1998)

38. *People v. Cornell*, 466 Mich 335 (2002); see also MCL §750.115 for a definition of the crime of breaking and entering without permission

39. *Ibid*

40. MCL §750.110a(5)

41. MCL §750.110a(6)

42. MCL §750.110a(7)

43. Another use of the term "burglary" is found in MCL §750.116, which codifies the crime of possession of burglar's tools.

44. *Uniform Crime Reports, op. cit.*

45. *People v. Cain*, 238 Mich App 95; 605 NW2d 28 (2000)

46. *People v. Pohl*, 202 Mich App 203; 507 NW2d 819 (1993), rem'd 445 Mich 918; 519 NW2d 899 (1994)

47. MCL §750.356(2)

48. MCL §750.356(3)

49. MCL §750.356(4)

50. MCL §750.356(5)

51. MCL §750.357

52. MCL §750.356(a)

53. MCL §750.357a

54. MCL §750.357b

55. MCL §750.358

56. MCL §750.359

57. MCL §750.364

58. MCL §750.365

59. *Uniform Crime Reports, op. cit.*

60. *Uniform Crime Reports, op. cit.*

61. MCL §750.71

62. MCL §750.74

63. MCL §750.75

64. *People v. Ayers*, 213 Mich App 708; 540 NW2d 791 (1995), lv den 452 Mich 877; 552 NW2d 173 (1996)

65. *People v. Barber*, 255 Mich App 288 (2003)

66. MCL §750.316(1)(b)

67. *People v. Reeves*, 202 Mich App 706; 510 NW2d 198 (1993), rem'd 448 Mich 1; 528 NW2d 160 (1995)

68. Recent issues of the FBI's *Hate Crime Statistics* may be viewed online on the FBI's website (http://www.fbi.gov/ucr/ucr.htm)

69. MCL§28.257a

70. Michigan State Police crime statistics reports - hate crimes (http://www.michigan.gov/msp)

71. *Ibid*

72. *Ibid*

73. *Ibid*

CHAPTER 4

THE POLICE IN MICHIGAN

INTRODUCTION

There are many levels of police agencies in America today, including federal law enforcement, state police, county sheriff's agencies, and city police. Currently, there are 613 separate law enforcement agencies in Michigan. The majority of these are township, village, or city departments, each of which has its own chief, its own organization, and its own policies and procedures. In addition, there are 83 county sheriff's departments, the Michigan State Police, and a wide variety of special-purpose law enforcement agencies at all levels of government. Currently, there are over 23,000 certified law enforcement officers in Michigan. The largest department in the state is the Detroit Police Department, with over 4,000 officers. There are 468 departments in Michigan that employ less than 29 officers.[1]

LOCAL POLICING

The majority of the police departments in Michigan are local or city departments. In most cases, the chief of each department is appointed by the head of the city's political system (city manager, mayor, commissioner, etc.) Because of this, it can be a very political position. If a new city manager is elected, the appointment of a new police chief often follows soon afterwards. Every local department is independent of every other department. The goals, purposes, and priorities vary greatly among departments, with each local agency responding to the needs and desires of the population it serves. All municipal police departments are full-service police agencies which provide a wide range of police services, including law enforcement, order maintenance, and service.

The Detroit Police Department

Detroit is the largest city in Michigan, with a population of 951,270 in 2000.[2] The **Detroit Police Department** (DPD) is responsible for policing the city of Detroit, which includes a total of 143 square miles. The department is divided into 13 precincts, which range in size from only 1.3 miles (the First Precinct) to 16 miles (the Sixth Precinct).[3] In 2001, the DPD employed 4,184 sworn officers and 666 civilian personnel. It is the largest police department in the state.[4]

Currently, the minimum entry requirements for the department include:

- be at least 18 years of age
- be a US citizen
- be a high school graduate or the equivalent (GED)

- have vision correctable to 20/20 in each eye and normal depth and color perception
- have a valid driver's license at the time of application
- have no felony convictions
- be capable of performing the essential duties and functions of the position of police officer

Applicants who meet the basic entry requirements must go through a variety of tests, including a written examination, a physical agility test, a medical and psychological examination, a background investigation and criminal history check, and several oral interviews.[5]

The Lansing Police Department

Lansing is the capital of Michigan and has a population of approximately 119,000. The **Lansing Police Department** (LPD) has 268 sworn officers and 101 civilian employees and is responsible for policing an area of approximately 33 square miles. The LPD is divided into two precincts, the North Precinct and the South Precinct.[6]

One of the more unique programs at the LPD is the **Mentor Program**. The program was developed after it was realized that over 40 percent of the department's sworn personnel had been hired during the four-year period 1992 through 1996. In 1997, the department implemented the Mentor Program as a way to allow senior officers to share their knowledge with junior officers, and as a way of increasing retention within the department. In 2001, the program was recognized by the U.S. Department of Justice as one of the country's "Best Practices." The program is not a substitute for the field training program that all new officers go through. Instead, it is designed to supplement the field training program and help new officers have a successful policing career. Participation in the program is voluntary, both for the mentor and protege, and the mentors go through a course of training before being assigned to a protege.[7]

Currently, the minimum entry requirements for the LPD include:

- must be at least 21 years of age on the date of appointment
- must be a U.S. citizen
- must have a valid Michigan driver's licence at time of employment
- must meet departmental physical requirements
- must have visual acuity of at least 20/100 uncorrected, correctable to 20/20 in each eye
- must have at least 90 quarter or 60 semester credits from an accredited college or university (in some cases, 53 quarter or 36 semester credits are acceptable), with a major in law enforcement preferred
- must have no felony convictions
- must have begun a Hepatitis B inoculation program at the Lansing Medical Facility prior to employment

Applicants who meet the minimum requirements go through a variety of tests, including a written examination, personality assessment test, psychological and medical examinations, background investigation, physical agility test, and oral board examination. In July 2003, new recruits earned an annual salary of $20,924 while in the academy. Academy graduates with 90 quarter or 60 semester credit hours had a starting salary of $34,133, while those with 180 quarter or 120 semester credits started at $36,744. Officers receive a step increase in pay yearly until reaching top pay.[8]

COUNTY POLICING

Each of the 83 counties in Michigan has a separate sheriff's department. The office of sheriff is mandated by the Michigan Constitution, which states that:

> There shall be elected for four-year terms in each organized county a sheriff, ... whose duties and powers shall be provided by law...[9]

Chapter 51 of the Michigan Consolidated Laws deals with the office of sheriff.

Sheriff's departments in Michigan are full service police agencies that provide police services to all unincorporated areas of the county. In addition, incorporated cities that do not wish to set up their own city police department may contract out to their county sheriff's department for police services. MCL §51.221 outlines the duties of sheriffs in Michigan, stating that:

> A sheriff, undersheriff, or deputy sheriff of a county of this state may serve or execute civil or criminal process issued by a court of this state, and have and exercise all the powers and duties of constables. Except where other fees are expressly provided, they shall be entitled to the same fees for these services as are allowed by law to constables in like cases.

Not only is the sheriff responsible for providing law enforcement services to the county, but s/he is also responsible for executing various civil and criminal processes, executing summons, orders, and judgments, and running the county jail.

The Wayne County Sheriff's Office

The **Wayne County Sheriff's Office** (WCSO) is the largest sheriff's department in the State of Michigan, with a total of 1,430 employees, including 1,075 sworn officers and 355 civilians in 2001.[10] Detroit, the largest city in Michigan, is located in Wayne County. The Sheriff is the chief law enforcement officer for Wayne County and is responsible for providing law enforcement services to the public, as well as being in charge of the county detention facility.[11]

WCSO is divided into several divisions. The **Field Services Division** is responsible for providing law enforcement services to unincorporated Wayne County. The Division's Marine Safety

Unit patrols all county waterways, including Lake Erie, Lake St. Clair, Belleville Lake, and the Detroit River. Other units within the Field Services Division include the Mounted Patrol, the Detective Bureau, and the Identification Bureau. The **Courts Division** maintains order in the various county courts as well as being responsible for transferring prisoners between the courts and the county jail. Other responsibilities of the Courts Division include serving warrants on individuals who are delinquent in child support payments, serving civil notices such as subpoenas, evictions, and divorce papers, and serving felony arrest warrants from the Third Circuit Court. The **Jail Division**, which is the oldest division in the department, is responsible for the three adult detention facilities in the county. Finally, the **Executive Division** is the administrative arm of the WCSO, as well as housing several special units, including the Drug Enforcement Unit, the Morality Unit, the Training Unit, the Community Services Unit, and Internal Affairs.[12]

The Oakland County Sheriff's Office

The **Oakland County Sheriff's Office** (OCSO) provides full service law enforcement to unincorporated Oakland County as well as serving 15 incorporated communities through law enforcement contracts. The department has approximately 1,200 employees and an annual budget of approximately $98 million. About 1.2 million people live in Oakland County; the OCSO is responsible for providing law enforcement services to over 273,000 of them.[13]

The OCSO is made up of six separate divisions. The **Administrative Services Division** is the human resource arm of the department, as well as being responsible for areas such as budget, accounting, and payroll. The **Patrol Services Division** provides law enforcement services throughout the county. The Division has contracts with 15 communities to provide services such as uniformed patrol, traffic enforcement, and school liaison officers. There are a number of special units within the Patrol Services Division. The Aviation Unit has two helicopters that are available to assist any police department in the county. The Marine Unit, which patrols the over 450 lakes in Oakland County, maintains over two dozen boats, a hovercraft, a number of snowmobiles, and has a fully-trained dive and rescue team. This unit also trains and certifies civilians in boating safety. The Parks Unit is responsible for law enforcement in a number of county parks as well as for the supervision of prisoner trustees participating on work details in the parks. The Alcohol Enforcement Team focuses on the problem of drunk driving on county roads. In 2000, a total of 288 drunk drivers were arrested by the team, and 99.5 percent of those arrested were convicted. In addition to law enforcement, the team is responsible for alcohol education and runs the S.C.O.P.E Program (Stop Drinking, Consider the Consequences, Observe Yourself, Protect Society, Educate Others) in Oakland County high schools.[14]

The **Emergency Response And Preparedness Division** was created after the terrorist attacks on September 11, 2001 and is the newest division in the OCSO. The Division works with other county law enforcement agencies, as well as the Michigan State Police and various federal agencies (such as the FBI, INS, Customs, and the Secret Service). The Division ensures that the county is prepared to respond to natural disasters (tornados, severe weather, etc.) as well as a variety of man-made emergencies (terrorism, weapons of mass destruction, hazardous materials, etc.) The

50

Technical Services Division deals with a variety of special crime-related issues and problems and provides support services for other law enforcement agencies. There are a number of special units within the Division, including crime scene investigation, narcotics enforcement, fire investigation, and computer crimes. The Division also houses the communications or dispatch unit, the records bureau, the OCSO crime laboratory, and the training unit.[15]

There are two separate divisions responsible for the supervision of inmates in the Oakland County correctional system. The **Corrective Services Division** is responsible for the majority of these inmates. The Division operates the Main Jail as well as supervising the Booking Unit, through which all inmates pass upon entry into the county correctional system. The **Corrective Services Satellite Division** is responsible for all inmates not under the jurisdiction of the Corrective Services Division. The majority of these inmates are housed in boot camps, trusty camps, or in the county's minimum security work release facility. The Satellite Division is under contract with the City of Southfield to operate the Southfield Detention Facility, which holds not only prisoners from Southfield but also most of the offenders arrested in Royal Oak Township. In addition, the Division is responsible for running the Frank Greenan Detention Facility, a medium-security jail that was designed to relieve overcrowding problems in the Main Jail. The Court Services Unit of the Division is responsible for providing security to the county courthouse building, for patrolling the County Complex, and for transporting prisoners to and from the court.[16]

STATE POLICING

There are two main types of **state police agencies** within the United States. Some states, such as North Carolina, separate or **decentralize** the functions and keep criminal investigations separate from the uniformed highway patrol. However, other states, including Michigan, operate a **centralized** or full-service state police agency which includes both highway patrol functions and criminal investigation.

The Michigan State Police

The **Michigan State Police** (MSP) was originally organized in 1917 as a temporary wartime constabulary agency designed to provide domestic security to the state during World War I. The department was made a permanent state agency in 1919. In 1921, Trooper Harold E. Anderson became the first MSP officer to die in the line of duty. Currently, it serves as the primary statewide law enforcement for the state of Michigan.[17]

Chapter 28 of the Michigan Compiled Laws deals with the Michigan State Police. According to MCL §28.2,

> There is created a department of the state government which shall be known and designated as the Michigan state police, which shall consist of a director as its executive head, and of such officers and employees as may be appointed or employed

in such department. The director shall be appointed by the governor, by and with the advice and consent of the senate, and shall hold office during good behavior. The salary of the director shall be such as shall be appropriated by the legislature. The director shall execute the constitutional oath of office.

In 2001, the MSP employed 3,233 persons including 2,129 certified officers and 1,104 civilians. Of the certified officers, 88 percent were male and 12 percent female. Of the civilian employees, 47 percent were male and 53 percent female.[18]

According to MCL §28.4, the MSP must include a uniformed division, a detective division, and any other divisions established by the commanding officer of the MSP. Currently, the MSP is composed of four main divisions, or bureaus. The **Office of the Director** is the organizational arm of the MSP. In addition to the Human Resources and Training Divisions, this office oversees the Office of Highway Safety Planning and the Emergency Management Division. The **Michigan Commission on Law Enforcement Standards** has been placed administratively under this bureau of the MSP. The **Administrative Services Bureau** is responsible for the day-to-day management of the MSP, as well as supervising various technical services. The Bureau houses the Communications Division, the Budget Office, and the MSP's Management Services Division. In addition, the Bureau's Criminal Justice Information Center (CJIC) is responsible for administering the state's Uniform Crime Reporting Program and for collecting data on traffic crash reports from law enforcement agencies statewide. The CJIC also maintains criminal history records, firearms records, crime analysis statistics, the state's Automated Fingerprint Identification System, and other record management systems.[19]

The **Uniform Services Bureau** is the uniformed division of the MSP that is mandated by statute. The bureau is divided into seven districts that include 63 separate posts. Six of these districts are in the lower peninsula while the seventh (District 8 - there is no District 4) comprises the whole of the state's upper peninsula. In addition to the uniformed patrol, the Bureau includes several divisions. The Motor Carrier Division is responsible for the regulation and enforcement of laws relating to commercial vehicles. Their activities include ensuring commercial vehicles obey traffic speed laws, detecting and apprehending offenders using commercial vehicles in the commission of a crime, identifying and intercepting any contraband transported on state roads (e.g., illegal drugs, alcohol, weapons), enforcing state laws and regulations relating to hazardous materials, investigating commercial vehicle crashes, and conducting safety inspections of school buses and commercial vehicles. The Special Operations Division supervises the MSP Operations Center, which serves as the department's command and control center. The Prevention Services arm of the division provides various protection services, including Michigan's Missing Child Information Clearinghouse and the school liaison officer program. The Aviation Section's five aircraft provide airborne support to law enforcement agencies throughout the state. The Field Support Section includes the MSP Canine Unit, the Underwater Recovery Unit, and the Emergency Support Team. The Traffic Services Section is responsible for all statewide traffic safety issues not under the auspices of the Motor Carrier Division.[20]

The **Investigative Services Bureau** is the detective division of the MSP that is mandated by statute. Detectives are assigned to one of the Bureau's divisions to provide a variety of investigative services to the MSP. The Field Detective Division includes those detectives who are assigned to work out of the 63 posts. These detectives are responsible for the general investigation of the majority of crimes assigned to the Bureau. Detectives in the Criminal Investigation Divisions work out of one of the MSP's various specialized task forces and investigative units. These Divisions also maintain the Arson Tip Line, Crime Stoppers Tip Line, and the Internet Safety Tip Line. Detectives working in the Fire Marshal Division investigate possible cases of arson and train local police and fire departments in arson investigation. The Forensic Sciences Division includes seven crime labs as well as ten polygraph testing offices and provides forensic laboratory services to law enforcement agencies throughout the state.[21]

MCL §28.4 outlines the minimum requirements for appointment as an MSP officer:

> ...All persons appointed as officers shall be at the time of their appointment not less than 21 years of age, the maximum age limit to be fixed by the commissioner from time to time, shall be of sound mind and body, be of good moral character, be citizens of the United States and residents of the state of Michigan and shall possess such educational qualifications as the commissioner may from time to time prescribe...

Currently, the MSP requires that all applicants must:

- be a U.S. citizen at the time of taking the written examination
- be at least 21 years of age at the time of taking the written examination
- be a high school graduate or the equivalent (GED)
- be a resident of the State of Michigan prior to graduating from the police academy and provide proof of residency
- have no felony convictions
- have a satisfactory driving record
- have a valid Michigan driver's license prior to appointment to the academy
- meet departmental physical requirements, including vision and hearing standards[22]

Applicants who meet the minimum requirements must first take the Michigan Civil Service Entry Level Law Enforcement Examination, which is administered by the Michigan Department of Civil Services. Only those applicants who pass the examination may continue in the selection process. Candidates must also pass the Michigan Commission on Law Enforcement Officer Standards Physical Strength & Agility Test, participate in a candidate orientation program, and complete a personal history questionnaire and an experience and education questionnaire. Candidates then go through a pre-screening interview to determine if they may continue in the selection process. A background investigation also is conducted on all qualified candidates to help to determine employment suitability. Candidates also go through a hiring interview and may then receive a conditional offer of employment, providing they successfully pass the remaining pre-employment tests. These include psychological screening, a medical examination, and drug screening.[23]

Candidates who pass all these pre-employment steps are assigned to a class at the academy. The academy training generally lasts 18 weeks and is a residential program, although recruits may return home on the weekends. After graduation from the academy, recruits may be assigned to any post in the state. As probationary troopers, they participate in a 17-week Field Training Officer program before being certified to work alone. The starting salary for a state trooper is $29,670.48. Troopers receive annual pay increases to a maximum salary of $46,103.04 after five years.[24]

POLICE TRAINING

Police departments today require highly-qualified and well-trained officers. In 1965, the Michigan Legislature created the **Michigan Commission on Law Enforcement Standards** (MCOLES). According to MCL §28.609(1),

> The commission shall promulgate rules to establish law enforcement officer minimum standards. In promulgating the law enforcement officer minimum standards, the commission shall give consideration to the varying factors and special requirements of local police agencies.....

These include physical, mental, educational, and moral minimum standards relating to the recruitment, selection, appointment, and certification of law enforcement officers in Michigan. The Commission also regulates officer training programs, mandating minimum instructional hours, attendance requirements, courses of study, and other basic training requirements. In addition, the Commission regulates the minimum amount and types of in-service training received by law enforcement officers in the state. Over 600 law enforcement agencies operate under standards set by the Commission, including state, county, and municipal police as well as specialized departments such as tribal, railroad, airport, and park police.[25]

The Commission is made up of fifteen members, as outlined in MCL §28.621. Twelve of these are appointed by the governor, with the advice and consent of the Senate:

- three persons chosen from a list of nine active voting members of the Michigan Association of Chiefs of Police submitted by the Association

- three persons chosen from a list of nine elected sheriffs submitted by the Michigan Sheriffs' Association

- one person selected from a list of three individuals submitted by the Prosecuting Attorneys Association of Michigan

- one person selected from a list of three individuals submitted by the Criminal Defense Attorneys of Michigan

- one person selected from a list of three individuals submitted by the Michigan State Police Troopers Association

- one person selected from a list of three individuals submitted by the Michigan Chapter of the Fraternal Order of Police

- one person selected from a list of three individuals submitted by the Police Officers Association of Michigan

- one person selected from a list of three individuals submitted by the Detroit Police Officers Association

These commissioners serve staggered three-year terms, so that no more than four terms expire in any given year. The other three members of the Commission serve because of their position in the government. They include:

- the Attorney General (or a designated representative)

- the Director of the Department of State Police (or a designated representative who is a Michigan State Police Officer)

- the Chief of a police department serving a city of more than 750,000 persons (or a designated representative who is a command-level officer within that department)

MCOLES has set minimum standards that must be met by anyone entering law enforcement in Michigan. These standards include:

- be at least 18 years of age
- be a citizen of the U.S.
- possess a high school diploma or GED
- have no prior felony convictions (unless expunged)
- have a good moral character (determined by a comprehensive background investigation, including school records, work records, personal traits, and any law violations, including traffic law convictions)
- have a valid Michigan driver's license
- be free from any physical disorders, diseases, or defects, or any mental or emotional disorders that may impair the individual's performance of the duties of a law enforcement officer or that might endanger the lives of the officer or of others

- meet specified hearing and vision standards, including normal color vision
- have height and weight appropriate in relation to each other
- be physically sound, including possessing all extremities and having no sensory impediment
- pass the MCOLES reading and writing examination and the MCOLES physical agility test, or approved agency equivalent examinations
- be examined by a licensed physician to ensure all medical standards are met
- be fingerprinted and be tested for the illegal use of controlled substances
- undergo an oral interview
- successfully complete the MCOLES mandatory basic training curriculum and pass the MCOLES certification examination[26]

These are minimum requirements. Any law enforcement agency may establish qualifications for employment that exceed these minimum requirements. For example, both the Lansing Police Department and the Michigan State Police require applicants to be at least 21 years of age upon appointment.[27]

In addition to mandating minimum entry requirements, MCOLES also develops basic training standards for law enforcement officers in Michigan. Currently, the mandatory minimum basic training program is 494 hours. Topics covered in the curriculum include investigation, criminal law, criminal procedure, patrol procedures, juveniles, detention procedures, first aid, firearms, traffic control and enforcement, emergency preparedness and disaster control, and many others. While all officers must go through and pass the minimum training program, any department is free to expand upon the program, add additional topics of study, and require additional instructional hours, above the mandatory minimum 494 hours of training.[28]

MCOLES is also responsible for awarding certification as a state law enforcement officer. To be certified, an individual must not only comply with all the minimum selection and training standards mandated by MCOLES but also pass a statewide certification examination and be employed as a law enforcement officer with a law enforcement agency in the state. If a certified officer resigned from his/her agency of employment, state certification will lapse after a period of time which is determined by the officer's time in service, but no more than two years after discontinuing service as a law enforcement officer. In addition to awarding certification, MCOLES also has the responsibility for revoking that certification if the officer has been convicted of a felony or has committed a fraud or misrepresentation in gaining certification.[29]

THE MICHIGAN POLICE CORPS

The federal **Police Corps Program** is:

designed to address violent crime by helping state and local law enforcement agencies increase the number of officers with advanced education and training assigned to community patrol. The program, which operates within states that have submitted an approved state plan, motivates highly qualified young people to serve as police officers and sheriffs' deputies in the municipalities, counties and states that need them most. It does this by offering Federal scholarships on a competitive basis to college students who agree to serve where needed on community patrol for at least four years.

The Police Corps reduces local costs of hiring and training excellent new officers. The Federal government pays for rigorous law enforcement training for each Police Corps participant...[30]

The **Michigan Police Corps** (MPC) is run by the Ferris State University Criminal Justice Institute. The program is designed to attract individuals to the field of policing in the state of Michigan. It primarily recruits college seniors who are full-time students enrolled in a baccalaureate program at an accredited university or college in the state. In some cases, graduate students may also be eligible for the MPC program. Applicants must meet all MCOLES requirements for law enforcement officers, must pass all stages of the MPC screening process, and be willing to accept a four-year assignment with a participating state law enforcement agency. The MPC attempts to match participants with the agencies of their choice but does not guarantee this. MPC participants generally spend all four years of their service commitment on community patrol. They have all the same rights and responsibilities as any other member of their agency and receive the same pay and benefits.[31]

Participants must attend a 20-week residential academy training program. MPC pays all associated costs, including room, board, equipment, and uniforms, and each participant receives a stipend of $250 per week while attending the academy. Participants who successfully complete the MPC academy training program and are hired by a participating agency are eligible for up to $30,000 of educational expense reimbursement. In addition, the hiring agencies also benefit. A law enforcement agency that employs MPC participants will receive $10,000 per participant for each year of required service.[32]

NOTES

1. Michigan Commission on Law Enforcement Standards - found on Michigan State Police home page under "Service to Governmental Agencies" (http://www.michigan.gov/msp)
2. Census and Statistical Data for Michigan (http://www.michigan.gov/census)
3. Detroit Police Department home page (http://www.ci.detroit.mi.us/police/default.htm)
4. Federal Bureau of Investigation (2002). *Crime in the United States - 2001.* (http://www.fbi.gov/ucr/01cius.htm)
5. Detroit Police Department home page, *op. cit.*
6. Lansing Police Department home page (http://www.lansingpolice.com/)

7. *Ibid*
8. *Ibid*
9. Michigan State Constitution, Article VII, §4
10. FBI, *op. cit.*
11. Wayne County Sheriff's Office home page (http://www.waynecounty.com/default_gov.htm)
12. *Ibid*
13. Oakland County Sheriff's Office home page (http://www.co.oakland.mi.us/sheriff/)
14. *Ibid*
15. *Ibid*
16. *Ibid*
17. Michigan State Police home page (http://www.michigan.gov/msp)
18. FBI, *op. cit.*
19. Michigan State Police home page, *op. cit.*
20. *Ibid*
21. *Ibid*
22. *Ibid*
23. *Ibid*
24. *Ibid*
25. Michigan Commission on Law Enforcement Standards home page, *op. cit.*
26. *Ibid*
27. Lansing Police Department and Michigan State Police home pages, *op. cit.*
28. Michigan Commission on Law Enforcement Standards home page, *op. cit.*
29. *Ibid*
30. Office of the Police Corps home page (http://www.ojp.usdoj.gov/opclee/)
31. Michigan Police Corps home page
    (http://www.ferris.edu/education/michiganpolicecorps/homepage.htm)
32. *Ibid*

CHAPTER 5

THE COURT SYSTEM IN MICHIGAN

INTRODUCTION

The Michigan court system works under the concept of "One Court of Justice". The criminal court system in the state is a two-tiered system, with two levels of appellate courts as well as several trial courts. The two appellate courts in Michigan are the state Supreme Court and the Court of Appeals. The trial courts include a circuit court, which serves as the trial court of general jurisdiction, as well as various courts of limited jurisdiction.[1]

FEDERAL COURTS IN MICHIGAN

There are a number of federal courts which sit in Michigan. These should not be confused with the state trial and appellate courts.

Although they are not specifically part of the Michigan State Court system, there are two **federal district courts** which sit in Michigan[2]. These are the Eastern District Court and the Western District Court, each with two divisions. These are the trial courts of the federal system, and are not related to the state district courts.

The **U.S. Courts of Appeals** are the intermediate appellate court of the federal court system and have appellate jurisdiction only over federal laws. Judges in these courts are nominated by the President of the United States and confirmed by the Senate. Michigan, along with Kentucky, Ohio, and Tennessee, is part of the Sixth Circuit[3]. The U.S. Court of Appeals is not related to the state court of appeal, although they are both appellate courts.

THE MICHIGAN SUPREME COURT

The **Michigan Supreme Court** is the state's highest court, and there is no further appeal in the state from the decisions of this court. Its decisions are binding upon all other courts in the state.

According to the Michigan State Constitution, the Supreme Court is made up of seven justices. All Supreme Court justices are elected by the qualified voters of the state and serve eight-year terms. Terms are staggered so that no more than two justices are elected in any given year.[4] Every two years, one of the seven justices is selected by the Court to serve as the chief justice.[5]

According to MCL §600.152, "The chief justice of the supreme court is the head of the judicial system."

To serve as a supreme court justice, an individual must have been authorized to practice law in Michigan for at least five years and must be under the age of 70 at the time of election.[6] The Michigan Supreme Court sits in Lansing. Term begins on August 1st and continues through July 31st of the following year.[7]

The Michigan Court Rules outlines the jurisdiction of the Supreme Court, stating that:

The Supreme Court may:

(1) review a Judicial Tenure Commission order recommending discipline, removal, retirement, or suspension...;
(2) review by appeal a case pending in the Court of Appeals or after decision by the Court of Appeals...;
(3) review by appeal a final order of the Attorney Discipline Board...;
(4) give an advisory opinion...;
(5) respond to a certified question...;
(6) exercise superintending control over a lower court or tribunal...;
(7) exercise other jurisdiction as provided by the constitution or by law.[8]

The majority of applications for appeal come from litigants who want the court to review a decision made by the Michigan Court of Appeals. The court has discretion to choose whether or not to accept an application for appeal. Of the over 2,000 "applications for leave to appeal" received annually, only approximately one hundred are granted by the Court. The majority of these deal with cases that involve issues of constitutional law, state statutory law, or other significant legal questions such as points of law over which the lower courts disagree. The rest of the applications are denied. A denial does not mean that the Court upholds or affirms a decision made by a lower court in the state, but only that the Court has decided not to hear the case.[9] The process by which an application for leave to appeal is made is outlined in MCR Rule 7.302. Decisions of the Michigan Supreme Court are published in the *Michigan Reports*.

In 2002, a total of 2,180 cases were filed in the Supreme Court. Of these, 61 percent were criminal cases and 39 percent were civil cases.[10]

THE MICHIGAN COURT OF APPEALS

The **Michigan Court of Appeals** is the state's intermediate appellate court of review. Prior to its creation in 1963, all appeals were heard by the Supreme Court. However, increasing problems of delay and congestion within the Supreme Court led to the development of the current two-tier appellate court system, with the Court of Appeals acting as a "buffer" between the lower trial courts and the Michigan Supreme Court. By handling the majority of the appellate work in the state, the

Court of Appeals allows the Supreme Court to review only those cases that raise important legal questions and to ensure that decisions made throughout the state are uniform. Today, the majority of cases which are appealed from the trial courts do not reach the Michigan Supreme Court but are reviewed by the Court of Appeals.

The Court of Appeals originally consisted of nine judges.[11] Over the years, the state legislature has increased this number to the present total of 28 judges.[12] The court sits in Lansing, Detroit, Grand Rapids, and Southfield. The requirements to serve as a Court of Appeals judge are the same as for a Supreme Court justice.[13] Like Supreme Court justices, judges of the Court of Appeals are elected by the voters, although they serve six-year terms.[14] The state is divided into four judicial districts for the purpose of electing judges to the Court of Appeals. A total of seven judges are elected from each district.[15]

Court of Appeals judges sit in panels of three and hear cases in Lansing, Detroit, Grand Rapids, and Marquette. The panels are rotated so that all judges hear cases in all four locations.[16] In 2002, a total of 7,156 cases were filed with the Michigan Court of Appeals, an increase of 0.8 percent over the previous year.[17] In most cases, the decision of the Court of Appeals represents the final appellate review of a litigated case and is therefore final, unless the cases is appealed to the Michigan Supreme Court.

MICHIGAN TRIAL COURTS

Circuit Courts

The **circuit court** is the state's trial court of general jurisdiction. According to the Michigan State Constitution,

> The circuit court shall have original jurisdiction in all matters not prohibited by law; appellate jurisdiction from all inferior courts and tribunals except as otherwise provided by law; power to issue, hear and determine prerogative and remedial writs; supervisory and general control over inferior courts and tribunals within their respective jurisdictions in accordance with rules of the supreme court; and jurisdiction of other cases and matters as provided by rules of the supreme court.[18]

Essentially, the circuit court has original jurisdiction over all criminal cases involving felony offenses as well as some serious misdemeanor offenses. In addition, the circuit court hears civil cases involving more than $25,000. The court has appellate jurisdiction over lower trial courts, such as the district court and the probate court.

The state is divided into 57 judicial circuits, each containing one or more counties. The number of judges per circuit is determined by the state legislature and listed in the Michigan Compiled Statutes.[19] Circuit court judges are elected and serve terms of six years.[20] The requirements to serve as a circuit court judge are the same as for a Supreme Court justice or Court of Appeals judge.[21]

Each judicial circuit has a **family division** of the circuit court.[22] The family division has jurisdiction over a variety of family-related matters, including adoptions, divorce, child support, child custody claims, paternity issues, juvenile delinquency proceedings, and child protection proceedings.[23]

In 2002, a total of 355,592 cases were filed in circuit court. Of these, approximately 67 percent were family division filings. A total of 60,415 cases were criminal filings. There were 6,337 appeals filed in 2002. The majority (56 percent) were administrative agency matters but there were 456 criminal appeals.[24]

District Courts

The **district court** was created by order of Article VI of the 1968 Michigan State Constitution and is a trial court of limited jurisdiction. According to MCL §600.8311, the criminal jurisdiction of the district court includes:

- Misdemeanors punishable by a fine or imprisonment not exceeding 1 year, or both.
- Ordinance and charter violations punishable by a fine or imprisonment, or both.
- Arraignments, the fixing of bail and the accepting of bonds.
- Preliminary examinations in all felony cases and misdemeanor cases not cognizable by the district court, but there shall not be a preliminary examination for any misdemeanor to be tried in a district court.

The district court also has original jurisdiction for all civil cases involving up to $25,000. Civil cases involving up to $3,000 may be heard in the small claims division of the district court. In these cases, the participants waive the right to be represented by an attorney, the right to a trial by jury, rules of evidence, and the right to appeal the decision of the district court judge. Both parties must agree to this or the case will be heard in the general civil division rather than the small claims division.[25] District court judges also have the authority to perform marriages.[26]

District judges are elected and serve six year terms. The requirements to serve as a district judge are the same as for those of other trial court judges.[27] In addition, the judge must be a registered voter in the district in which s/he is elected.[28]

District court judges have the authority to appoint district court magistrates. District court magistrates have the power to issue search and arrest warrants, arraign arrested suspects and set bail, accept guilty pleas for some crimes, and pass sentence on certain violations, including traffic violations. If the magistrate is licensed to practice law in Michigan, s/he may hear cases in the small claims division of the district court.[29]

In 2002, there were a total of 430,921 non-traffic filings in district courts in Michigan. Approximately 18 percent of these were felony filings, 74 percent were misdemeanor filings, and 8 percent were civil infractions. There were also 2,236,197 traffic filings in district court.[30]

Municipal Courts

After the passage of the 1968 Michigan State Constitution, the majority of **municipal courts** were converted to district courts. However, five districts in Macomb and Wayne Counties still retain a municipal court.[31] Municipal courts have civil jurisdiction over cases involving claims of up to $1,500, or up to $3,000 *if the local funding unit approves.* They have similar criminal jurisdiction as the district court. To be a municipal judge, an individual must be a resident and voter of the municipality and must be licensed to practice law in Michigan. Municipal judges serve terms of six years. In 2002, a total of 34,846 cases were filed in municipal court.[32]

COURT ADMINISTRATION

The State Court Administrative Office

According to the Michigan State Constitution,

> ...The supreme court shall appoint an administrator of the courts and other assistants of the supreme court as may be necessary to aid in the administration of the courts of this state. The administrator shall perform administrative duties assigned by the court.[33]

The **State Court Administrative Office** (SCAO) is responsible for the administration of trial courts in Michigan. This includes providing management support for probate, district, and circuit courts in Michigan. Tasks include establishing and implementing performance standards for the courts, implementing Supreme Court administrative policies, providing technical assistance and support staff, collecting and analyzing a wide variety of court-related data, ensuring caseflow management proceeds in an efficient manner, developing and approving court forms, and developing court-related publications for use by the general public. The SCAO is also responsible for managing the Michigan Drug Treatment Court Program. The SCAO's **Office of Dispute Resolution** is in charge of developing and coordinating various alternative dispute resolution options and services within the legal system. The **Access to Justice Program** is designed to locate and remove barriers relating to race, ethnicity, gender, economic status, language, or disability. A main goal of the program is to improve citizen access to the Michigan courts.[34]

The State Bar of Michigan

The **State Bar of Michigan** was created in 1935 by order of the state legislature. The membership of the State Bar consists of everyone who is licensed to practice law in the state. Members of the State Bar are officers of the court.[35] The State Bar is supervised by the Michigan Supreme Court. According to MCL §600.904,

> The supreme court has the power to provide for the organization, government, and membership of the state bar of Michigan, and to adopt rules and regulations

concerning the conduct and activities of the state bar of Michigan and its members, the schedule of membership dues therein, the discipline, suspension, and disbarment of its members for misconduct, and the investigation and examination of applicants for admission to the bar.

The State Bar is run by a Board of Commissioners made up of no less than 31 and no more than 33 members. The 2002-2003 Board is composed of 32 members, including five elected officers: the President, President-Elect, Vice President, Secretary, and Treasurer. Ten members of the Board, including the five elected officers, serve on the Executive Committee and run the State Bar between meetings of the full Board. In addition to the Board, the State Bar also has an organization known as the Representative Assembly, which is responsible for policy development. The Assembly was created by the Supreme Court in 1971, at the request of the State Bar, as a way of increasing the number of members actively participating in making policy for the Bar. The Assembly is structured so that it reflects the population of bar members from each of the state's judicial districts. Currently, there are 150 elected members.[36]

The responsibilities of the State Bar include:

- conducting character and fitness investigations of potential members to ensure they meet minimum professional standards

- conducting investigations and prosecutions of individuals who are illegally practicing law in the state

- participating in the review and evaluation of new state laws and court rules

- administering a **Client Protection Fund**, which reimburses individuals who have been victimized by a lawyer who has misappropriated funds entrusted to him or her

As of September, 2002, there were a total of 34,982 active members of the State Bar, as well as 1,117 affiliated members (these include law students, legal assistants, and legal administrators). Annual dues for active members are $160 and have not been increased since 1994.[37]

Anyone wishing to practice law in Michigan must be a member of the State Bar. The Michigan Supreme Court has outlined the requirements for individuals applying for admission to the State Bar. They include:

- must be at least 18 years of age
- must be of good moral character
- must have completed at least 60 semester or 90 quarter hours towards an undergraduate degree from an accredited college or university before entering law school

- must have a JD, LLB, or LLM degree from a reputable and qualified law school that is incorporated in the U.S. or its territories, and that requires at least 3 years of full-time or four years of part-time study

Applicants must pass the Multistate Professional Responsibility Examination (MPRE) with a scaled score of 75 or greater. In addition, applicants also must pass the Michigan Bar Examination with a combined score of at least 135. However, under some conditions, lawyers who are already licensed to practice in another state in the U.S. or in another country may be eligible for admission to the State Bar without having to take the Michigan Bar Exam.[38]

MICHIGAN CRIMINAL COURT PROCEDURES

The basic procedures involved in a criminal trial, including the pretrial activities, are similar in most states. In Michigan, the process begins when the police are notified (or in some other way discover) that a crime has been committed and they initiate an investigation into that crime. The procedures discussed in this section apply specifically to felony offenses; however, the procedures for misdemeanors are extremely similar.

Arrest and Booking

After the police have determined both that a crime has in fact been committed and that a specific person committed the crime, they may place that individual under **arrest**. In some situations, the police may have obtained a **warrant for arrest** from a magistrate. The warrant includes a statement of the crime of which the suspect is accused as well as an order directing a law enforcement officer to take the person into custody and bring him or her before a magistrate to answer to the charges made against him or her.[39] MCL §764.1a describes when a warrant for arrest may be issued. However, in Michigan (as in most states), the majority of arrests are made by police officers acting without a warrant. MCL §764.15 outlines those situations in which it is lawful for an officer to make an arrest without a warrant.

After a suspect has been arrested and taken to the county jail, s/he undergoes the **booking** or **police processing** procedure, which involves entering into the police record various facts about the suspect. At this time, the suspect will be photographed and fingerprinted and may be placed in a police lineup.

Arraignment

The first stage of the court process is known as the **arraignment**. This is generally held before a magistrate, but may also be before a district court judge. During the arraignment, the magistrate will inform the defendant of the charges against him or her (and of the possible penalties) and of his or her constitutional rights. The magistrate will also determine whether the defendant has retained counsel or, if s/he is indigent and cannot afford to hire an attorney, has had counsel assigned. If an indigent defendant has not had an attorney assigned, the magistrate will appoint one at this time.

The magistrate will also consider whether or not the defendant is entitled to any form of **pretrial release**, including **bail**. Although the U.S. Supreme Court stated in *Stack v. Boyle*[40] that the U.S. Constitution does not guarantee the right to bail, the Michigan State Constitution does guarantee bail for most offenders, stating that

> ...All persons shall, before conviction, be bailable by sufficient sureties, except that bail may be denied for the following persons when the proof is evident or the presumption great:
> (a) A person who, within the 15 years immediately preceding a motion for bail pending the disposition of an indictment for a violent felony or of an arraignment on a warrant charging a violent felony, has been convicted of 2 or more violent felonies under the laws of this state or under substantially similar laws of the United States or another state, or a combination thereof, only if the prior felony convictions arose out of at least 2 separate incidents, events, or transactions.
>
> (b) A person who is indicted for, or arraigned on a warrant charging, murder or treason.
> ©) A person who is indicted for, or arraigned on a warrant charging, criminal sexual conduct in the first degree, armed robbery, or kidnapping with intent to extort money or other valuable thing thereby, unless the court finds by clear and convincing evidence that the defendant is not likely to flee or present a danger to any other person.
> (d) A person who is indicted for, or arraigned on a warrant charging, a violent felony which is alleged to have been committed while the person was on bail, pending the disposition of a prior violent felony charge or while the person was on probation or parole as a result of a prior conviction for a violent felony.[41]

The Constitution also states that if a defendant is denied bail, they must be brought to trial within 90 days of the denial of bail. If this is not done, a bail hearing must be scheduled and bail be granted.[42]

A number of factors are considered by a magistrate in determining whether a defendant should be granted pretrial release. These include:

- the nature and seriousness of the charge against the defendant

- the need to protect the public

- the defendant's prior criminal record and the dangerousness of the defendant

- factors that may affect the likelihood that the defendant will appear at the trial.[43]

The magistrate has several options when allowing pretrial release. These include:

- releasing the defendant on his or her personal recognizance, with a written promise to appear and without requiring any money to be paid

- releasing the defendant on a cash bond, requiring the defendant to pay the full amount of the bond to the court

- releasing the defendant on a ten percent bond, requiring the defendant to pay the ten percent of the total amount of the bond to the court as a guarantee of appearance (if the defendant fails to appear, the court will require the remainder of the bond to be paid)

- releasing the defendant on a surety bond, which is a promise made by an approved bondsman that the defendant will appear as required.[44]

In some cases, the magistrate also may impose conditions on the bond, such as requiring the defendant to have no contact with the victim.

If the defendant fails to return to court as promised, all bond money will be forfeited. Even if the defendant does appear, the money or property that was posted for the bond is not always returned at the end of the case. The court may apply the money to outstanding court costs, fees, or fines.

At the arraignment, the defendant may be asked to make an initial **plea** to the charges. A defendant has five possible plea options in Michigan:

- not guilty
- guilty
- *nolo contendere* ("no contest")
- guilty but mentally ill
- not guilty by reason of insanity[45]

A plea of *nolo contendere* indicates that, while not admitting guilt, the defendant does not contest the charges. This plea may only be made with the consent of the court.[46] A defendant may only enter a plea of guilty but mentally ill or not guilty by reason of insanity with the consent of the court and the prosecutor.[47]

Preliminary Examination

During the arraignment, the magistrate will set a date for a **preliminary examination**. Unless the defendant waives his or her right to this hearing, it must be scheduled no more than 14 days after the arraignment.[48] The preliminary examination, which is sometimes known as a **probable cause hearing**, is generally conducted by a district court judge. The purpose of the preliminary examination is to ensure that the state has enough evidence to proceed with the case against the defendant. The defendant has a right to be represented by counsel at this hearing.

During the preliminary examination, the prosecution presents witnesses and evidence to the judge. The defense has the right to cross-examine prosecution witnesses and to present its own evidence and witnesses as well. At the conclusion of the preliminary examination, the judge must take one of three actions

1. If the judge finds sufficient probable cause to charge the defendant with the crime, or a lesser included felony offense, the judge must bind the defendant over to circuit court for trial.

2. If the judge finds no probable cause regarding the charged felony offense, but does find probable cause for a lesser misdemeanor offense that is under the jurisdiction of the district court, s/he may set the case for trial in district court.

3. If the judge determines that there is not sufficient probable cause to charge the defendant with a crime, the case must be dismissed.[49]

Circuit Court Arraignment

After a felony case is sent to the circuit court, the defendant is arraigned a second time. This is a brief hearing before a circuit court judge. At this time, the defendant is once again advised of his or her constitutional rights, given formal notice of the charges that are being filed against him or her, and enters a plea to the charge. The formal charging document is known as an **information** and a copy is given to the defendant or the defendant's attorney. The defendant may waive his or her right to an arraignment.[50]

Pre-Trial Conference

After the arraignment, some judges may call for a meeting between the judge, the defense attorney, and the attorney prosecuting the case. Depending on the individual judge, the conference may be held either in open court or in the judge's chambers. One of the topics that is frequently discussed at a pre-trial conference is the issue of **plea bargaining**. While plea bargaining is not a formal stage of the criminal justice process, it is an extremely important process in every state, including Michigan. In general, a plea bargain means that the if defendant agrees to plead guilty or

no contest to a charge, the prosecutor will reciprocate in some way. Possible actions by the prosecutor in exchange for a plea of guilty or no contest include:

- the prosecutor will not file charges against the defendant
- the prosecutor will dismiss charges against the defendant
- the prosecutor will move for the dismissal of additional charges against the defendant
- the prosecutor will recommend a specific sentence
- the prosecutor will not oppose a specific sentence requested by the defense

Pre-Trial Motions

There are a number of **pre-trial motions** that may be filed in court. A **motion to dismiss** is filed by the defense and asks that the case against the defendant be dismissed. Possible grounds for dismissal include:

- the statute of limitations has expired

- the defendant has been tried on these charges (double jeopardy)

- the defendant was granted immunity from prosecution

- the defendant's right to a speedy trial was denied

- the defendant's constitutional rights were violated in such a way that irreparable damage was done to the defendant's case preparation

A **motion to continue** requests that the case be delayed for a specific period of time. This may be filed by either the defense or the prosecution. A **motion to suppress evidence** considers whether evidence was obtained illegally (e.g., through an unlawful search and seizure) and should therefore be prohibited from use as evidence in court.

A **motion for a change of venue** requests that the location of the trial be changed on the grounds that it is not possible to obtain a fair and impartial trial in the county where the case is currently pending because there is a significant prejudice against the defendant. In response to this motion, the judge has the option to transfer the case to the circuit court of another county.[51]

The Right to a Speedy Trial

The Michigan State Constitution and the Michigan Compiled Laws guarantee all individuals accused in a criminal proceeding the right to a speedy trial.[52] This means that each case must be brought to trial within a certain specified period of time. If the defendant has been denied bail by the

courts, s/he must be brought to trial no more than 90 days after the date on which bail was denied. If the trial has not begun by this time (unless the defendant is responsible for the delay), the court is required to schedule a bail hearing and set bail for the defendant.[53]

The Michigan Compiled Laws do not specify a specific time after which the defendant's right to a speedy trial may be considered to have been violated. If the defendant has been granted bail, a four-pronged test is used by the courts to respond to such a claim. The four elements of the test include:

1. The length of the delay
2. The reason(s) for the delay
3. The defendant's assertion of his or her right to a speedy trial
4. Possible prejudice to the defendant's case[54]

The Michigan courts have discussed some of these elements in detail. For example, if the defendant was responsible for delays in bringing the case to trial, these delay periods are not grounds for dismissing the case because of a violation of the right to a speedy trial. The courts have held that delays that are caused by the functioning of the court system itself, such as a crowded docket, are given only minimal weight or consideration, and may not necessarily deprive the defendant of a speedy trial.[55]

The responsibility is on the defense to claim that his or her right to a speedy trial was violated. The courts have held that the failure of a defendant to assert his or her right to a speedy trial, and to claim that this right was violated, in a timely fashion, will weigh against a finding by the court that the defendant's right to a speedy trial was violated.[56] However, it does not automatically mean that the court will find against the defendant.

Finally, the court will examine the length of the delay and the possible prejudice that the delay may have on the defendant's case. The courts have held that if the trial has been delayed for less than 18 months, the defendant is responsible for showing that the case has been prejudiced. However, if the trial has been delayed for more than 18 months, prejudice to the defendant's case is presumed and the burden of proof is on the prosecutor to show that the defendant was not prejudiced by the delay.[57] Long delays do not automatically violate the defendant's right to a speedy trial. For example, in the case of *People v. Cain*[58], the court held that, based on the circumstances of the case, a 27-month delay between arrest and trial did not violate the defendant's constitutional right to a speedy trial.

Trial

The vast majority of criminal cases are disposed of by a plea of guilty on the part of the defendant. However, if the defendant enters a plea of not guilty and the case does go to **trial**, the procedure is similar regardless of whether the case involves a felony or a misdemeanor.

According to the Sixth Amendment to the U.S. Constitution, all defendants have the right to a speedy, public, and impartial trial. The Michigan State Constitution also guarantees the right to a **jury trial** in all criminal cases.[59] In Michigan, felony criminal cases are tried before a twelve-member jury and the verdict must be unanimous before the defendant may be found guilty of any charge.[60]

The basic steps involved in a circuit court trial in Michigan are discussed in both the Michigan Compiled Laws and the Michigan Court Rules.[61]

Jury Selection

The first step in a trial is the **selection of the jury**. A *venire*, or list of possible jurors, is compiled from a state list of licensed drivers. The process of jury selection is known as *voir dire* and involves an examination of the prospective jurors by the court and by the attorneys for both the prosecution and the defense. The purpose of the *voir dire* is to determine whether each potential juror is impartial and will be able to render a fair verdict in a case. Potential jurors are placed under oath and then questioned by the judge, prosecutor, and defense counsel.

During the *voir dire* process, both the defense and the district attorneys are allowed to make challenges, or to object to the inclusion of certain potential trial jurors. Like most states, Michigan allows two types of challenges to prospective jurors. **Challenges for cause** generally are based on the attorney's belief that the juror is biased in some way that will prevent him or her from acting impartially and without prejudice during the trial. According to MCR 2.511(D), a challenge for cause may be made if the prospective juror:

(1) is not qualified to be a juror;
(2) has been convicted of a felony;
(3) is biased for or against a party or attorney;
(4) shows a state of mind that will prevent the person from rendering a just verdict, or has formed a positive opinion on the facts of the case or on what the outcome should be;
(5) has opinions or conscientious scruples that would improperly influence the person's verdict;
(6) has been subpoenaed as a witness in the action;
(7) has already sat on a trial of the same issue;
(8) has served as a grand or petit juror in a criminal case based on the same transaction;
(9) is related within the ninth degree (civil law) of consanguinity or affinity to one of the parties or attorneys;
(10) is the guardian, conservator, ward, landlord, tenant, employer, employee, partner, or client of a party or attorney;
(11) is or has been a party adverse to the challenging party or attorney in a civil action, or has complained of or has been accused by that party in a criminal prosecution;
(12) has a financial interest other than that of a taxpayer in the outcome of the action;
(13) is interested in a question like the issue to be tried.

Peremptory challenges may be used by either attorney to remove potential jurors from the jury panel without giving specific reasons. A juror is who peremptorily challenged is excused from jury services without cause. Each defendant is allowed by right a total of five peremptory challenges unless the crime with which s/he is charged is punishable by life imprisonment. In that case, a defendant being tried alone is entitled to 12 peremptory challenges. If a defendant is being tried jointly, the number of peremptory challenges to which s/he is entitled depends on the number of co-defendants in the case. The prosecutor is entitled to the same number of peremptory challenges as a defendant being tried alone or the total number of peremptory challenges to which all defendants are allowed. In addition, the court has the option of granting additional peremptory challenges to either the defense or the prosecution, or both.[62]

After the selection of the jury is completed, the jurors are impaneled and sworn in by the clerk of the court. The **Oath of Jurors** in Michigan states that:

> You shall well and truly try, and true deliverance make, between the people of this state and the prisoner at bar, whom you shall have in charge, according to the evidence and the laws of this state; so help you God.[63]

However, any juror is allowed to make an **affirmation** instead of taking the oath, by substituting the phrase "This you do under the pains and penalties of perjury" for the last four words of the oath.[64]

Opening Statements

In Michigan, the prosecutor is required to make an **opening statement** to the court. This statement consists of an overview of the prosecution's case and the facts that the prosecutor intends to prove to the court. After the prosecution's opening remarks are completed, the defense may make an opening statement as well, either immediately after the prosecution's statement or immediately before beginning to present evidence for the defense. However, unlike the prosecution, the defense opening statement is optional. The court has the right to limit the length of the opening statements.[65]

Presentation of the Prosecution's Evidence

After the opening statements are completed, the prosecution begins to present evidence in support of the charge that has been brought against the defendant. The prosecution presents first because the state is bringing the charge against the defendant and, because of the presumption of innocence, has assumed the burden of proof. Evidence submitted into court may include witness testimony, documents, and physical objects of various types. The judge determines the admissibility of each piece of evidence, based on the criteria set forth in the Michigan Rules of Evidence (MRE). These rules are intended primarily to ensure that unreliable evidence, or evidence that was illegally obtained, is not accepted into court.

The prosecutor generally begins with **direct examination** of the prosecution's first witness, who is obviously expected to give evidence to support the state's case against the defendant. After the prosecutor finishes questioning the witness, the defense is allowed to **cross-examine** the same witness. If the prosecutor wishes, s/he may then return to ask the witness more questions in a process known as **re-direct examination**. Following this, the defense attorney has the option to question the

witness once more during the **re-cross examination**. This procedure is repeated for each witness called by the prosecution.

Presentation of the Defense's Evidence

After the prosecution has presented all its evidence and called all its witnesses, the defense may then offer evidence. Unlike the state, the defense is not required by law to offer evidence at trial. If the defense attorney chose not to make an opening statement at the start of the trial, s/he may make one prior to presenting evidence.

In many cases, the defense will begin by putting forth a motion for dismissal, on the grounds that the evidence offered by the prosecution was insufficient to sustain a conviction. If the motion is denied, the defense presents its evidence.

The procedure for the presentation of the evidence by the defense is similar to that of the prosecution: direct examination, cross examination, re-direct, and re-cross. The defendant is not required to testify at any point in the trial; both the Fifth Amendment to the U.S. Constitution and Article 1, §17 of the Michigan State Constitution protect the defendant against self-incrimination.

Rebuttal and Surrebuttal

After the defense has presented its evidence, each side is given the opportunity to offer rebuttal evidence relating to the evidence presented by the opposing party. The judge may also allow the presentation of new evidence. In general, the prosecutor first presents a **rebuttal**, possibly including additional evidence that may nullify or challenge that presented by the defense, after which the defense is given the opportunity to present a **surrebuttal** case.

Closing Arguments

Once all the evidence is presented, each side is given the opportunity to make a **closing argument** which is addressed directly to the jury. The prosecutor has the right to make the first closing argument, after which the defense has the option of presenting closing arguments as well. If the defense presents an argument, the prosecution has the right to present a rebuttal argument limited only to those issues raised in the argument made by the defense.[66]

During this stage of the trial, each attorney reviews and summarizes the evidence that best supports his or her side of case, discusses any inferences that may be drawn from that evidence, and points out weaknesses in the opponent's case. Closing arguments are optional and either or both sides may waive their right to make a closing presentation.

Instructions to the Jury

The judge is required to provide instructions to the jury regarding any legal issues or points of law which are applicable to the case. In most cases, this is done after the closing arguments but if both parties consent, the court may instruct the jury before closing arguments are made.[67] This step is also known as **charging the jury**. During this stage, the judge provides the jury with detailed legal information about the crimes charged and the process of deliberation.

Jury Deliberation and Verdict Rendition

After the judge has charged the jury, the jury retires to the jury room for **deliberation**. At this time, the jurors discuss the case and attempt to come to agreement on a verdict concerning the guilt or innocence of the defendant. In Michigan, all jurors must unanimously agree on a guilty verdict before the defendant can be convicted of the charge.[68] If the jurors are unable to agree on a verdict after a reasonable period of time, they are **deadlocked** and considered to be a "**hung jury**." If this happens, the judge will declare a **mistrial** and the case may have to be retried in front of a new jury.[69]

If the jurors come to an agreement on a **verdict**, they are returned to the courtroom and the verdict is read in open court. Either the defense or the prosecution is entitled to request a poll of the jury to ensure that each member of the jury agrees with the verdict and that no member was coerced or intimidated into agreeing, or agreed simply out of exhaustion. If any juror responds negatively, the court must refuse to accept the verdict and direct the jury to resume deliberations. The judge also has the right to require the jury to be polled.[70]

If the verdict of the jury is not guilty, the trial is over and the defendant must be immediately discharged from custody and is entitled to the return of any bail money and the exoneration of any sureties. The trial court judge is required to accept a verdict of not guilty. Because of the constitutional protections against double jeopardy, the defendant may never be tried in state court for those same charges.

Proceedings Between the Verdict and the Sentence

If the defendant is found guilty, he/she will be sentenced. However, after a verdict of guilty is rendered and before the sentencing phase of the trial, the defendant may make a **post-trial motion** to set aside or modify the verdict. If the judge sets aside the verdict, the defendant may be entitled to a dismissal, a reduction of the charges, or a new trial. These motions are rarely granted.

During this time the probation department will prepare a **pre-sentence report** for the judge. The report includes a summary of the crime as well as providing information on the defendant's background and criminal history. The victim may be given the option to make a victim impact statement and the probation department includes a recommended sentence in the report.

The Sentence

If the defendant is found guilty, s/he will be sentenced by a judge. The judge must follow the Michigan Sentencing Guidelines if s/he is handing down a sentence of incarceration. Other sentencing options include fines, probation, community service, restitution, or some combination of these. The sentencing process is discussed in more detail in Chapter 6.

Appeal

If the defendant is convicted of a crime, s/he may have the option of **appealing** the conviction. Appeals from the Circuit Court are heard in the Michigan Court of Appeals. In some cases, the prosecution may also have the right to appeal a verdict of not guilty, although this is a much less

common occurrence.[71] An appeal does not involve retrying a case or re-examining the factual issues surrounding the crime; it only involves an examination or review of the legal issues involved in the case. The primary purpose of an appeal is to make certain that the defendant received a fair trial and that he or she was not deprived of any constitutional rights at any time. Unless the decision is modified by the Michigan Supreme Court, the decision of the Court of Appeals is final.[72]

NOTES

1. Michigan State Constitution, Article VI, §1
2. See 28 U.S.C. 102
3. The Federal Judiciary home page (http://www.uscourts.gov/)
4. Michigan State Constitution, Article VI, §2
5. MCR Rule 7.323
6. Michigan State Constitution, Article VI, §19(2) and §19(3)
7. MCR Rule 7.301(B)
8. MCR Rule 7.301(A)
9. Michigan Courts homepage - Michigan Supreme Court (http://courts.michigan.gov/supremecourt)
10. Michigan Supreme Court 2002 Annual Report (http://courts.michigan.gov/scao/resources/publications/statistics/2002execsum.pdf)
11. Michigan Sate Constitution, Article VI, §8
12. MCL §600.301
13. Michigan Sate Constitution, Article VI, §19(2) and §19(3)
14. Michigan Sate Constitution, Article VI, §9
15. MCL §600.302
16. Michigan Courts homepage - Michigan Court of Appeals (http://courtofappeals.mijud.net/)
17. Michigan Supreme Court 2002 Annual Report, *op. cit.*
18. Michigan State Constitution, Article VI, §13
19. See MCL §600.501 through §600.549i
20. Michigan Sate Constitution, Article VI, §12
21. Michigan State Constitution, Article VI, §19(2) and §19(3)
22. MCL §600.1003
23. MCL §600.1021
24. Michigan Supreme Court 2002 Annual Report, *op. cit.*
25. Michigan Courts homepage - Trial Courts (http://courts.michigan.gov/trialcourts/trial.htm)
26. MCL §600.8613
27. Michigan State Constitution, Article VI, §19(2) and §19(3)
28. MCL §600.8201
29. Michigan Supreme Court 2002 Annual Report, *op. cit.*
30. *Ibid*

31. As of September 1, 2003, the five remaining municipal courts are located in Grosse Point, Grosse Pointe Park, Grosse Pointe Woods, and Grosse Pointe Farmes (all located in Wayne County) and Eastpoine (located in Macomb County).
32. Michigan Supreme Court 2002 Annual Report, *op. cit.*
33. Michigan State Constitution, Article VI, §3
34. Michigan Courts homepage - State Courts Administrative Office (http://courts.michigan.gov/scao/)
35. MCL §600.901
36. State Bar of Michigan homepage (http://www.michbar.org/)
37. State Bar of Michigan Annual Financial Report for fiscal year ending September 30, 2002 (available on the State Bar of Michigan homepage, *op. cit.*)
38. State Bar of Michigan homepage, *op. cit.*
39. MCL §764.1b
40. *Stack v. Boyle*, 342 U.S. 1 (1951)
41. Michigan State Constitution, Article I, §15
42. *Ibid*
43. MCL §765.6(1)
44. MCR Rule 6.106
45. MCR Rule 6.301(A)
46. MCR Rule 6.301(B)
47. MCR Rule 6.301(C)
48. MCL §766.4
49. MCL §766.13
50. MCR Rule 6.113
51. MCL §762.7
52. Michigan State Constitution, Article I, §20 and MCL §768.1
53. Michigan State Constitution, Article I, §15
54. *People v Gilmore*, 222 Mich App 442; 564 NW2d 158 (1997)
55. *Ibid*
56. *People v Wickham*, 200 Mich App 106; 503 NW2d 701 (1993)
57. *People v. Holtzer*, 255 Mich App 478 (2003)
58. *People v. Cain*, 238 Mich App 95; 605 NW2d 28 (1999)
59. Michigan State Constitution, Article I, §20
60. MCR Rule 6.410
61. See MCL §768.1 *et.seq.* And MCR Rule 6.414
62. MCR Rule 6.412(E)(1)
63. MCL §768.14
64. MCL §768.15
65. MCR Rule 6.414(B)
66. MCR Rule 6.414(E)
67. MCR Rule 6.414(F)
68. MCR Rule 6.410
69. MCR Rule 6.420

70. *Ibid*
71. MCL §770.12
72. MCR Rule 7.201(D)

CHAPTER 6

SENTENCING IN MICHIGAN

INTRODUCTION

After a criminal defendant pleads guilty or is found guilty in court by a judge or jury, the judge must impose a **sentence** of punishment upon the offender. A sentence is a penalty imposed on a defendant for the crime of which the defendant has been adjudicated guilty or to which the defendant has pled guilty or no contest. According to the courts,

> The ultimate goal of sentencing is to protect society through just and certain punishment reasonably calculated to rehabilitate. The public must be protected from dangerous criminals who commit heinous and violent crimes, regardless whether the defendant is a juvenile or an adult.[1]

It is clear that there are multiple goals or objectives in sentencing, including the protection of society, punishment of the offender, and rehabilitation. These may at times conflict with one another, so that an attempt to meet one objective may make it difficult, or even impossible to also meet another objective. When this occurs, it is clear that in Michigan, the primary goal of sentencing is the protection of society.

In every case in which a conviction has been entered, the court is required to pronounce sentence. If the defendant has been found guilty on multiple counts, the court must pronounce sentence on each count.

TYPES OF SENTENCES

A variety of sentences may be imposed upon convicted offenders in Michigan. Sentences acceptable in the Michigan courts include:

- fines
- house arrest and/or electronic monitoring
- community service
- residential or non-residential probation
- residential or non-residential drug treatment
- incarceration in a jail or prison

Combinations of these sentences are also allowed. For example, a judge may order both imprisonment and a fine, or place an offender on probation and order the offender to engage in community service. However, the judge has only a limited amount of discretion when imposing a sentence as s/he is required to work within the sentencing guidelines that have been developed by the state legislature.

WHEN SENTENCING OCCURS

A sentencing hearing is held shortly after the defendant pleads guilty or *nolo contendere* to a criminal charge or is found guilty of a criminal charge at trial.[2] At this hearing the judge will impose a sentence. Prior to the sentencing hearing, the probation department will conduct a **pre-sentence investigation** (PSI) which is used by the judge when determining the final sentence. PSI reports must be prepared in all cases where the offender was charged with a felony offense, and may be prepared for misdemeanor offenders if requested by the court.[3] The PSI report includes:

- the offender's personal and criminal history
- a description of the circumstances of the crime
- information about the impact of the crime on the victim
- a written victim impact statement (if provided by the victim)
- a written statement by the offender (if provided)
- the probation officer's evaluation of the offender
- a sentencing recommendation[4]

CONCURRENT VERSUS CONSECUTIVE SENTENCES

If an offender is convicted of multiple offenses at the same time, the court has the option of ordering sentences of imprisonment to run consecutively or concurrently. **Concurrent sentences** are served at the same time while **consecutive sentences** are served in succession, one after the other. If multiple sentences are served concurrently, the controlling sentence is the longest one.[5] The decision to impose consecutive rather than concurrent sentences is an important one as it can significantly increase the overall length of the offender's sentence. In general, judges tend to impose consecutive sentences in cases that involve multiple distinct offenses and/or victims, in cases where the offender was on probation at the time of the current offense, and in cases where the offender's prior record was particularly bad.

In some cases, the court is required to order multiple sentences be served consecutively. For example, if an offender commits a crime while incarcerated in a Michigan penal institution, is convicted of that crime, and is sentenced to an additional term of imprisonment, this new term may not begin to run until the original term of imprisonment has ended. The same holds true if an offender commits a crime after escaping from a Michigan penal institution.[6]

MICHIGAN SENTENCING GUIDELINES

Sentencing guidelines basically establish mandatory minimum and maximum sentences for specific crimes, which the judges are required to follow. Michigan has developed a system of sentencing guidelines for all felony offenses and all misdemeanor offenses that are punishable by incarceration for more than one year.[7] The state began developing sentencing guidelines in 1979, when the Supreme Court appointed an advisory committee to design a system of sentencing guidelines. In 1983, the guidelines were put into use on a voluntary basis and in 1984 their use became mandatory.

Use of the sentencing guidelines is a six-step process, which is outlined in the Michigan Sentencing Guidelines Manual.[8] Step 1 involves determining the crime group into which the offense for which the offender is being sentenced falls. The Michigan sentencing guidelines divide crimes into six main offense groups:

1. Crimes against a person
2. Crimes against property
3. Crimes that involve a controlled substance
4. Crimes against the public order
5. Crimes against the public safety
6. Crimes against the public trust

Step 2 involves determining the offenders "Prior Record Score" using the seven prior record variables (PRV):

1. PRV 1: prior high severity felony convictions
2. PRV 2; prior low severity felony convictions
3. PRV 3: prior high severity felony juvenile adjudications
4. PRV 4: prior low severity felony juvenile adjudications
5. PRV 5: prior misdemeanor convictions or prior misdemeanor juvenile adjudications
6. PRV 6: relationship to the criminal justice system
7. PRV 7: subsequent or concurrent felony convictions

Each PRV has several categories, each of which has a specific number of points associated with it. For example, PRV 1 considers the number of prior high severity felony convictions. An offender with one such prior conviction receives 25 points, an offender with two prior convictions receives 50 points, and an offender with three or more prior convictions receives 75 points. An offender with no prior high severity felony convictions receives 0 points. Prior Record Variables 2 through 5 also assign points based on the number of prior convictions or adjudications of various types that occurred within the past ten years.[9] PRV 6 focuses on the offender's relationship with the criminal justice system and assigns various numbers of points to offenders who are on probation or parole, incarcerated in jail awaiting adjudication or sentencing, or serving a sentence of incarceration. PRV

7 relates to offenders who have been convicted of multiple felony counts or who were convicted of a felony after the sentencing offense was committed. PRV 7 is the only variable that relates to current and subsequent convictions; the other six apply only to prior convictions.[10]

The third step involves determining the offense variable score. Offense variables (OV) are used to determine the seriousness of the offense for which the offender is being sentenced. There are a total of 19 OVs listed in the sentencing guidelines:

1. aggravated use of a weapon
2. lethal potential of the weapon possessed
3. physical injury to a victim
4. psychological injury to a victim
5. psychological injury to a member of the victim's family
6. intent to kill or injure another individual
7. aggravated physical abuse
8. victim asportation or captivity
9. number of victims
10. exploitation of a vulnerable victim
11. criminal sexual penetration
12. contemporaneous felonious criminal acts
13. continuing pattern of criminal behavior
14. offender's role
15. aggravated controlled substance offenses
16. property obtained, damaged, lost, or destroyed
17. degree of negligence exhibited
18. operator ability affected by alcohol or drugs
19. threat to the security of a penal institution or court or interference with the administration of justice.

Each OV has several categories, each with a specific associated number of points. For example, OV 1, the aggravated use of a weapon, has five categories. If a firearm was discharged at a person or a victim was cut or stabbed, the offender is assigned 25 points. If a firearm was pointed at the victim or the victim was threatened with a knife or other cutting or stabbing weapon, the offender is assigned 15 points. If the victim was touched with any other type of weapon, the offender is assigned 10 points. If a weapon was displayed or implied, the offender is assigned 5 points. If no aggravated use of a weapon occurred, the offender is not assigned any points.[11] Not all OVs are used for every offense. The actual OVs scored depend on the crime group into which the sentencing offense falls. For example, for crimes against property, only OVs 1-4, 9, 10, 12-14, 16, and 19 are scored.[12]

Step four involves determining the crime class and grid for the sentencing offense. There are nine crime classes, each with a separate grid from which the appropriate minimum sentencing range may be obtained. The nine crime classes are:

• Murder II	Punishment is life or any term of years.
• Class A Crimes	Crimes for which a sentence of up to life imprisonment may be appropriate.
• Class B Crimes	Crimes for which a sentence of up to twenty (20) years imprisonment may be appropriate.
• Class C Crimes	Crimes for which a sentence of up to fifteen (15) years imprisonment may be appropriate.
• Class D Crimes	Crimes for which a sentence of up to ten (10) years imprisonment may be appropriate.
• Class E Crimes	Crimes for which a sentence of up to five (5) years imprisonment may be appropriate.
• Class F Crimes	Crimes for which a sentence of up to four (4) years imprisonment may be appropriate.
• Class G Crimes	Crimes for which a sentence of up to two (2) years imprisonment may be appropriate.
• Class H Crimes	Crimes for which jail or other intermediate sanctions may be appropriate.[13]

The Michigan Sentencing Guidelines Manual includes a table of crimes with the associated crime group and class. For example, first degree criminal sexual conduct falls into the crime group of crimes against persons and crime class A. Breaking and entering with intent to commit a felony or larceny falls into the crimes against property group and crime class C.[14]

Step five involves determining the proper sentence range for the sentencing offense. This is done by locating the cell at the intersection of the OV and PRV levels on the appropriate crime class grid. The cell contains the guideline sentence range in months (or life in prison). For example, an offender with 25 OV points and 25 PRV points who has committed third degree criminal sexual conduct, a Class B offense, should receive a minimum sentence of 57-95 months incarceration in a state prison. If the statute defining a specific offense includes a statutory maximum sentence the minimum sentence imposed should not be more than two-thirds of the statutory maximum.[15]

A habitual offender may receive an enhanced sentence. If the offender is being sentenced for a second felony, the upper limit of the recommended minimum sentence range may be increased by 25 percent. If the offender is being sentenced for a second felony, the upper limit of the range may be increased by 50 percent. If the offender is being sentenced for a third felony, the upper limit may be increased by 100 percent.[16]

There are three different types of cells found in the sentencing grids. If the offender falls into a **prison cell**, the sentence will be a term of incarceration. If the offender falls into a **straddle cell** in the grid, either a minimum prison sentence or an intermediate sanction that may include a jail term of up to one year is an appropriate sentence. If the offender falls into an **intermediate sanction cell**, an intermediate sanction that may include a jail term of up to one year, or the maximum number of months listed in the cell (whichever is less), is an appropriate sentence. Intermediate sanctions are all lawful punishments other than imprisonment in a state prison facility. Examples of intermediate sanctions include:

- inpatient or outpatient drug treatment
- probation, conditional probation, or residential probation
- mental health treatment or counseling
- substance abuse counseling
- jail, jail with work/education release, jail with day parole
- community service
- payment of a fine
- house arrest and/or electronic monitoring

The sixth and final step involves the possibility of departing from the sentencing guidelines. According to MCL §769.34(3),

> A court may depart from the appropriate sentence range established under the sentencing guidelines set forth in chapter XVII if the court has a substantial and compelling reason for that departure and states on the record the reasons for departure. All of the following apply to a departure:
> - The court shall not use an individual's gender, race, ethnicity, alienage, national origin, legal occupation, lack of employment, representation by appointed legal counsel, representation by retained legal counsel, appearance in propria persona, or religion to depart from the appropriate sentence range.
> - The court shall not base a departure on an offense characteristic or offender characteristic already taken into account in determining the appropriate sentence range unless the court finds from the facts contained in the court record, including the presentence investigation report, that the characteristic has been given inadequate or disproportionate weight.

A departure is a sentence that does not fall within the appropriate minimum sentencing range established by the sentencing guidelines. However, there are some sentences that fall outside of a specific cell range that are not departures. These include:

1. when a mandatory minimum sentence is required,
2. when the cell exceeds the two-thirds limitation,
3. when a jail sentence is below a cell range in an intermediate sanction cell, and
4. when a jail sentence is below a cell range in a straddle cell.[18]

If a judge departs from the appropriate sentence range and imposes a more severe sentence, the judge is required to state the reasons for the departure and notify the defendant that s/he has the right to appeal the sentence.[19] If the defendant does appeal the sentence, and the court of appeals finds that the trial court did not have sufficient justification for the departure, the case is remanded to the sentencing judge, or another trial court judge, to be resentenced.[20]

VICTIM RIGHTS AND SERVICES

The Rights of Victims of Crime

In 1985, the state legislature passed the **Crime Victim's Rights Act** (CVRA).[21] The CVRA focused on the rights of crime victims, including the rights of victims to be notified and to participate in all states of the criminal justice process. The CVRA is extensive and provides for a wide variety of victims rights. These include:

- the right of the victim to be notified about his/her rights as a victim
- the right to prompt return of the victim's property
- the right to be notified if the defendant has been released from custody prior to trial
- the right to be notified of the procedures of the criminal process and of all court proceedings
- the right (when possible) to a victim waiting area in the court that is separate from the defendant and his/her family, relatives, and defense witnesses
- the right of the victim to be present at trial if s/he is not going to be called as a witness
- the right to make a written or oral victim impact statement to the probation officer for use in the preparation of the presentence investigation report
- the right to restitution
- the right to be notified if the offender is released or escapes from confinement

The CVRA is divided into three articles. The first focuses on the rights of victims of felony offenses, the second on the rights of victims of juvenile offenses, and the third on the rights of victims of serious misdemeanors. Articles 2 and 3 were added to the CVRA in 1988.

Essentially, a major result of the CVRA is that it requires law enforcement agencies, prosecutors, courts, the Michigan Department of Corrections, and various other criminal justice agencies to include victims of crime in the proceedings of the criminal justice system. These proceedings include criminal investigation, judicial proceedings, sentencing, and post-sentencing proceedings.

In 1988, the Michigan State Constitution was amended to include a **Declaration of Rights**, which lists a number of basic rights to which all victims of crimes in Michigan are entitled. The Constitution states that:

(1)   Crime victims, as defined by law, shall have the following rights, as provided by law:

The right to be treated with fairness and respect for their dignity and privacy throughout the criminal justice process.

The right to timely disposition of the case following arrest of the accused.

The right to be reasonably protected from the accused throughout the criminal justice process.

The right to notification of court proceedings.

The right to attend trial and all other court proceedings the accused has the right to attend.

The right to confer with the prosecution.

The right to make a statement to the court at sentencing.

The right to restitution.

The right to information about the conviction, sentence, imprisonment, and release of the accused.

(2) The legislature may provide by law for the enforcement of this section.

(3) The legislature may provide for an assessment against convicted defendants to pay for crime victims' rights.[22]

There were several reasons why the Michigan State Constitution was amended to include a listing of the rights of crime victims, even though these rights were already provided for by statute in the CVRA. First, the amendment created a balance between the rights of criminal defendants, which were already guaranteed in the state constitution, and those of crime victims. Second, the amendment made the rights of crime victims more permanent, as the effort involved in repealing a constitutional amendment is significantly greater than removing the CVRA from the state statutes. Finally, the amendment specifically provides a means by which these rights may be enforced.[23]

Under the CVRA, a victim is defined as any of the following:

(I) An individual who suffers direct or threatened physical, financial, or emotional harm as a result of the commission of a crime, except as provided in subparagraph (ii), (iii), or (iv).

(ii) The following individuals other than the defendant if the victim is deceased:

(A) The spouse of the deceased victim.

(B) A child of the deceased victim if the child is 18 years of age or older and sub-subparagraph (A) does not apply.

(C) A parent of a deceased victim if sub-subparagraphs (A) and (B) do not apply.

(D) The guardian or custodian of a child of a deceased victim if the child is less than 18 years of age and sub-subparagraphs (A) to (C) do not apply.

(E) A sibling of the deceased victim if sub-subparagraphs (A) to (D) do not apply.

(F) A grandparent of the deceased victim if sub-subparagraphs (A) to (E) do not apply.

(iii) A parent, guardian, or custodian of a victim who is less than 18 years of age and who is neither the defendant nor incarcerated, if the parent, guardian, or custodian so chooses.

(iv)   A parent, guardian, or custodian of a victim who is mentally or emotionally unable to participate in the legal process if he or she is neither the defendant nor incarcerated.[24]

Victim Impact Statements

A **victim impact statement** is a written report or verbal statement that is given to the sentencing judge or jury for consideration when sentencing the defendant. Such a statement includes admissible evidence concerning the impact or effects of the crime upon the victim. As noted above, one of the basic rights of all crime victims, as stated in the Michigan State Constitution, is the right to make a statement to the court at the sentencing of the accused offender. Victim impact statements may be made at two points in the sentencing process. First, MCL §780.764 states that

> The victim has the right to submit or make a written or oral impact statement to the probation officer for use by that officer in preparing a presentence investigation report concerning the defendant... A victim's written statement shall upon the victim's request, be included in the presentence investigation report.

If the crime victim has died, the victim's next of kin is entitled to the rights of the victim, including the right to make a victim impact statement.[25] The victim's impact statement to the prosecutor may include:

(a) An explanation of the nature and extent of any physical, psychological, or emotional harm or trauma suffered by the victim.
(b) An explanation of the extent of any economic loss or property damage suffered by the victim.
(c) An opinion of the need for and extent of restitution and whether the victim has applied for or received compensation for loss or damage.
(d) The victim's recommendation for an appropriate sentence.[26]

Second, the victim (or his or her next of kin) also has the right to appear in person at the sentencing hearing and make a statement to the court.[27] Information included in an oral impact statement generally focuses on the following issues:

- how the crime affected the victim and his or her family
- the emotional impact of the crime
- the financial impact of the crime
- possible concerns of the victim for the safety and security of the victim and his or her family
- what the victim would like to see as an outcome of the sentencing hearing

While all victims have the right to a victim impact statement, no victim is required to present such a statement. The victim's choice not to present a statement may not affect the decisions made at the sentencing hearing.

The Right to Restitution

According to both the Michigan State Constitution and the CVRA, all crime victims have the right to receive **restitution**.[28] MCL §780.766(2) states that:

> Except as provided in subsection (8), when sentencing a defendant convicted of a crime, the court shall order, in addition to or in lieu of any other penalty authorized by law or in addition to any other penalty required by law, that the defendant make full restitution to any victim of the defendant's course of conduct that gives rise to the conviction or to the victim's estate.

In addition to this statute, which is located in the felony article of the CVRA, restitution is also ordered in the juvenile and misdemeanor articles of the Act. Thus, restitution is essentially mandatory in Michigan. Restitution generally involves requiring the offender to pay a sum of money to the victim as reimbursement for injuries or damages due directly to the crime. In some cases, restitution may also be in a nonmonetary form (e.g., service to the community or to the victim).

According to the courts, the purpose of restitution is to compensate the victim for his or her losses and attempt to return the victim to his or her pre-victimization state, rather than to punish the defendant or juvenile.[29]

According to MCL §780.767 (and other sections of the CVRA), "in determining the amount of restitution to order... the court shall consider the amount of the loss sustained by any victim as a result of the offense." Losses that may be considered include:

- lost income resulting from the crime
- the cost of medical or psychological services
- the cost of rehabilitation, physical therapy, or occupational therapy required by the victim
- the cost of funeral expenses and related services, if the crime resulted in the death of the victim

If the crime resulted in the damage, loss, or destruction of the victim's property, the court must order the property be returned to the owner. If it is not possible or practical to return the property, or if return would be inadequate, the court must order the defendant to pay the value of the property at the time it was lost or damaged or the value of the property on the date of sentencing, whichever is greater.

The Right to Compensation

In addition to restitution, innocent victims of crimes committed in Michigan may be eligible for **victim compensation**. Michigan began offering victim compensation in 1976, becoming the 17th state to do so. Compensation differs from restitution in two ways. First, it is awarded by an administrative agency, rather than a court. Second, because restitution is a sentence and consists of money paid to the victim by the offender, it is only available if the offender has been prosecuted and convicted. Compensation is available to the victim even if the offender is never apprehended. Victim compensation is discussed in the **Crime Victims Compensation Act.**[30] Compensation is designed to assist eligible crime victims who are attempting to obtain financial assistance for out-of-pocket losses that are a direct result of a violent crime.

The Crime Victim Compensation Program in Michigan is administered by the **Crime Victims Services Commission** (CVSC). The CVSC is under the Michigan Department of Community Health and is responsible for providing a variety of services to crime victims. The Commission is made up of five members who are appointed by the governor. Of these, one member must be an attorney, one a prosecuting attorney, one must be a peace officer, one must be a doctor, and one must be a community-based victim advocate.[31]

MCL §18.354(1) provides a list of individuals who are eligible to apply for and claim an award of compensation. They include:

(a) A victim or an intervenor of a crime.;
(b) A surviving spouse, parent, grandparent, child, sibling, or grandchild of a victim of a crime who died as a direct result of the crime.
(c) Any other person dependent for his or her principal support upon a victim of a crime who died as a direct result of the crime.

In addition, the individual claiming compensation must have incurred at least $200 in out-of-pocket expenses or at least two continuous weeks of lost earnings or support. These limitations may be waived if the claimant is retired or a victim of first, second, or third degree criminal sexual conduct.[32]

There are four main categories of individuals who are not eligible to receive compensation awards from the CVSC. The first category includes any individual who is in some way criminally responsible for the crime upon which the compensation claim is based. Thus, an offender who is in some way injured during the commission of a crime may not apply for compensation as a result of that injury.[33] The second category includes an individual who was an accomplice to the crime.[34] Third, individuals who will gain a substantial and unjust economic benefit as a result of a compensation award are ineligible for compensation.[35] Finally, an individual who was confined as an inmate in a correctional institution at the time of the victimization is not eligible to receive compensation for his or her victimization.[36]

Only certain losses may be compensated by the victim compensation program. These include loss of support and out-of-pocket expenses. Loss of support refers to the loss of "actual monetary payments made by a victim or intervenor to or for a person principally dependent on the victim or intervenor."[37] An out-of-pocket loss is defined as:

> the unreimbursed and unreimbursable expenses or indebtedness reasonably incurred for medical care, psychological counseling, replacement services, any nonmedical remedial treatment rendered in accordance with a recognized religious method of

healing, or other services necessary as a result of the injury upon which a claim is based.[38]

By limiting out-of-pocket losses to those which are unreimbursed and unreimbursable, the legislature has made the victim compensation program a victim's "last resort." No other sources of reimbursement must be available for the victim to be eligible for compensation. All bills must first be filed with insurance companies before applying for compensation. Thus, for example, if the victim has adequate health insurance, s/he may not request compensation for medical expenses that are covered by that insurance. In addition, if the victim receives restitution from the offender to cover certain losses (e.g., lost income due to injury as a result of the crime), the victim may not also receive victim compensation for the same financial losses.

The statute lists the specific types of out-of-pocket expenses that are eligible for compensation. Medical care includes not only the cost of the actual care but also in some cases the cost of travel to and from a health care facility if the specific type of treatment is not available at a local facility. Replacement services refers to the cost of tasks that were performed by the victim prior to the crime but, because of the injury to the victim, must be performed by some other person. Examples of replacement services include child care, housekeeping and homemaking activities, and transportation.[39] Other services may include any recognized medical treatment, equipment, or supplies that the victim may require because of some physical injury or disability that is a direct result of the crime. In addition, MCL §18.361(3) specifies that certain funeral expenses may be eligible for compensation, including burial expenses and grief counseling. Expenses that are not directly related to the funeral services, such as the cost of flowers, catering services, headstones, or travel costs of family members attending the funeral, may not be compensated.

Not all crimes are eligible for compensation. In Michigan, awards of compensation are only given for economic losses and are only awarded for criminally injurious conduct (e.g., violent crimes). The victim compensation program will not compensate a victim for losses that resulted from a crime of theft, or for the loss of personal property (or damage to property), or for nonmonetary losses such as pain, suffering, and inconvenience. Thus, to the compensation program, a "victim" is an individual who, as the direct result of a criminal action, has suffered a personal physical injury.[40]

For an award of compensation to be considered, it must be shown that:

- a crime was committed
- the crime resulted in personal physical injury or death to a victim
- the crime was reported promptly to a law enforcement agency (generally within 48 hours)
- the victim was not incarcerated in a correctional facility at the time of the crime[41]

In most cases, a claim for compensation must be filed no more than one year after the crime occurred. However, there are some exceptions to this, and the CVSC also may extend the filing period for good cause.[42] Examples of good cause for extensions include:

- the delay in filing a claim was due to the victim's physical or emotional inability, where that inability was related to the criminal injury.

- the victim was not informed of the filing deadline by the appropriate authorities.

- the victim was given incorrect or incomplete information regarding compensation from the appropriate authorities.

- the victim consciously chose not to file a claim but later discovered that the injury or loss due to the crime was significantly greater than was originally known (for example, the victim originally believed that certain expenses were covered by medical insurance and later discovers that the expenses will not be reimbursed by the insurance company).

After the victim files a claim, the CVSC must conduct a review to determine if the victim is eligible and if compensation should be awarded. However, in some cases, when the crime resulted in severe immediate financial hardship, the CVSC may make an emergency compensation award prior to its final decision. The amount of an emergency award may not exceed $500 and will be deducted from any final award granted by the CVSC. If the amount of the final award is less than the emergency award, the victim must repay the excess to the CVSC.[43]

Unlike some states, Michigan uses a **serious financial hardship standard** when deciding whether a victim should be given compensation. According to MCL §18.361(7),

> If the commission finds that the claimant will not suffer serious financial hardship as a result of the loss of earnings or support and the out-of-pocket expenses incurred as a result of the injury if he or she is not granted financial assistance, the commission shall deny the award...

Essentially, the state's goal is to allow the victim to maintain a reasonable standard of living after the crime. If losses due to the crime will significantly lower the victim's standard of living, serious financial hardship is considered to exist. If the losses do not represent a financial hardship to the victim, compensation will be denied.

Another reason for denying an award of compensation is the victim's failure to cooperate with, or deliberate interference with, the criminal prosecution of the offender.[44] In addition, if the victim's misconduct in some way contributed to the victim's injury, the CVSC may reject a compensation claim, or reduce the amount of compensation awarded. Misconduct may include behavior on the part of the victim that provoked the crime.[45] An award may be reduced if the victim receives payments from other sources as a result of the injury. Such payments may include restitution payments from the offender, insurance payments, payments from public funds, or (as noted above), emergency compensation awards.[46]

There are limits to the amount of compensation that may be awarded. Currently, the maximum award in Michigan is $15,000 per claimant.[47]

NOTES

1. *People v. Cheeks*, 216 Mich App 470; 549 NW2d 584 (1996), lv den 454 Mich 866; 560 NW2d 633 (1997)
2. MCR Rule 6.425(D)(2)
3. MCL §771.14(1)
4. MCR Rule 6.425(A)
5. *Lickfeldt v Department of Corrections*, 247 Mich App 299 (2001)
6. MCL §768.7a(1)
7. Michigan Sentencing Guidelines Manual, 2003 edition
   (http://www.courts.michigan.gov/mji/resources/sentencing-guidelines/sg.htm)
8. *Ibid*
9. MCL §777.50
10. Specifics as to the number of points associated with each PRV category are defined in MCL §777.51 *et seq.* and in the Michigan Sentencing Guidelines Manual, *op. cit.*
11. Specifics as to the number of points associated with each OV category are defined in MCL §777.31 *et seq.* and in the Michigan Sentencing Guidelines Manual, *op. cit.*
12. MCL §777.22 and Michigan Sentencing Guidelines Manual, *op. cit.*
13. Michigan Sentencing Guidelines Manual, *op. cit.*
14. Crime group and class information may also be found in MCL §777.11 *et seq.*
15. MCL §769.34(2)(b) and Michigan Sentencing Guidelines Manual, *op. cit.*
16. MCL §777.21(3)
17. Michigan Sentencing Guidelines Manual, *op. cit.*
18. *Ibid*
19. MCL §769.34(7)
20. MCL §769.34(11)
21. MCL §780.751 *et seq.*
22. Michigan State Constitution, Article I, §24
23. Van Regenmorter, W. (1989). Crime victims' rights: A legislative perspective. 17 *Pepperdine Law Review* 59, 77.
24. MCL §780.752(1)(j)
25. *Ibid*
26. MCL §780.763(3)
27. MCL §780.765
28. Michigan State Constitution, Article I, §24 and MCL §780.766
29. *People v Grant*, 455 Mich 221, 230 n 10 (1997); *People v Law*, 459 Mich 419, 424 (1999); *People v Carroll*, 134 Mich App 445, 446 (1984)
30. MCL §18.351 *et seq.*
31. MCL §18.352

32.   MCL §18.354(3)
33.   MCL §18.354(2)
34.   *Ibid*
35.   MCL §18.361(8)
36.   MCL §18.360(d)
37.   MCL §18.351(h)
38.   MCL §18.351(e)
39.   MCL §18.351(g)
40.   MCL §18.351(I)
41.   MCL §18.360
42.   MCL §18.355
43.   MCL §18.359
44.   MCL §18.356(2)
45.   MCL §18.361(6)
46.   MCL §18.361(5)
47.   MCL §18.361(1)

CHAPTER 7

CAPITAL PUNISHMENT IN MICHIGAN

During the 18th and early 19th centuries, Michigan used the **death penalty** as a punishment for various violent crimes. However, in 1846, the Michigan legislature abolished **capital punishment** in the state. The ban became official on March 1, 1847, eliminating the death penalty for all crimes except for treason against the state. With the passage of this prohibition, Michigan became the first English-speaking government in the world to abolish capital punishment. International Death Penalty Abolition Day currently is observed on March 1, in remembrance of this anniversary. Today, Michigan is one of twelve states in the U.S. (plus the District of Columbia) that do not have the death penalty.

Throughout the state's history, there were a number of attempts to restore the death penalty and, conversely, to include the prohibition in the state constitution. It was not until 1963 that the state incorporated its prohibition on capital punishment into the state constitution. At that time, the ban was expanded to include the crime of treason. Article IV §46 of the Michigan State Constitution is entitled "Death Penalty" and specifically states, "No law shall be enacted providing for the penalty of death." Currently, the penalty for capital crimes is a mandatory sentence of life imprisonment with no possibility of parole. Only the state governor can commute this sentence.

Since the passage of the 1963 constitutional prohibition of the death penalty, there have been several attempts to repeal the ban on capital punishment in Michigan. Citizen groups have made multiple attempts to authorize the death penalty by referendum but none of these attempts ever made it to the ballot.[1] During the early 1990s, support for such a repeal was over 70 percent. However, according to a recent poll, support for the death penalty had shrunk to only 55 percent of Michigan residents by May 2001.[2]

In 2002, a number of Michigan police chiefs and politicians began a new attempt to bring back the death penalty to Michigan. The move was sparked by the deaths of three Detroit police officers in that year and originally focused only on imposing death as a punishment for the crime of killing first responders (police, firefighters, and paramedics). The campaign was later expanded to all first degree murders.[3] Among the groups supporting the return of capital punishment in Michigan is the Michigan Association of Chiefs of Police. A total of 400,000 signatures are required for the referendum to be placed on the 2004 ballot.[4]

NOTES
1. *Michigan in Brief: 1998-99.* (http://www.michiganinbrief.org/edition06/index.htm)
2. Hill, James G. (2001, May 14) "Poll shows fewer in state favor capital punishment." *Detroit Free Press.* (http://www.freep.com/news/mich/poll14_20010514.htm)

3.   Masson, John and Bill Laitner (2002, August 30), "Police chiefs pursue death penalty: Constitutional move follows cop killings." *Detroit Free Press* (http://www.freep.com/news/mich/cap30_20020830.htm)

4.   Neal, Adam L. (2002). "Association pushes death penalty." *Oakland Post.* (http://www.oakland.edu/post/091802/local.htm)

CHAPTER 8

CORRECTIONS IN MICHIGAN

THE MICHIGAN DEPARTMENT OF CORRECTIONS

The **Michigan Department of Corrections** (MDOC) oversees the operation of all state adult correctional facilities in Michigan. It was created in 1991 by Executive Order.

The first correctional organization in Michigan was the State Prison Commission which was created in 1921 and was one of five commissions under the supervision of the State Welfare Department. In 1936, the governor appointed a committee to study the prison system of Michigan. The committee wrote the Reform Act of 1937, which established a Department of Corrections and replaced the Prison Commission with a Corrections Commission. The law was revised again in 1953, with the passage of the Department of Corrections Act.[1] This act created the current MDOC and established the **Michigan Corrections Commission** (MCC) to administer the MDOC. Members of the MCC were appointed by the governor with the advice and consent of the senate.

In 1991, Governor Engler passed Executive Reorganization Order Number 1991-12. As a result, the MCC was eliminated and its authority and responsibility were transferred to the Director of the MDOC. The Director of the MDOC is appointed by the governor of Michigan and serves as its chief administrative officer.[2]

The MDOC is divided into several divisions or administrations, each headed by a deputy director. The **Correctional Facilities Administration** is responsible for inmates in all prisons and camps, as well as for the intake and evaluation process that all inmates go through when first sentenced to prison. The **Field Operations Administration** (FOA) provides probation and parole supervision throughout the state as well as supervising the Special Alternative Incarceration Program (boot camp). FOA is also responsible for the administration of the Michigan Parole Board, the Office of Community Corrections, and various other community residential programs. The **Administration and Programs Administration** is responsible for the daily organization of the MDOC. It includes purchasing, research and planning, budget preparation, information systems management, operations research and planning, and prisoner services. In addition, it is responsible for supervising Michigan State Industries and the Bureau of Health Care Services. There are several other units which report to the MDOC director as well. These include the **Executive Bureau**, the **Office of Audit, Internal Affairs and Litigation**, and the **Bureau of Human Resources**.[3]

At the end of 2002, the MDOC employed almost 18,000 staff, including over 9,000 corrections officers. The agency's authorized budget during the 2002 fiscal year was $1.6 billion.[4]

PRISONS IN MICHIGAN

Prisons in Michigan are run by the MDOC. At year end 2002, there were 49,489 inmates in the state's prisons and camps, an increase of 4.5 percent over the previous year. This number does not include offenders on probation or parole, or those resident in community residential programs. Of these inmates, 54 percent were black, 42 percent were white, and 3.5 percent were American Indians, Hispanics, and Asians. There are 42 prisons and 11 camps in the system, all under the supervision of the Correctional Facilities Administration.[5]

Prison Security Levels

Each prison facility in the state is given an individual **security level** designation. There are six custody levels, ranging from Level I (the lowest) through Level VI (the highest). The higher the level of security, the more restrictive the confinement and the more separated offenders are from the community outside the facility. **Secure Level I** facilities house offenders who are considered to be a fairly low security risk. These offenders may have committed violent crimes but do not pose serious management problems for the MDOC. An example of a Secure Level I facility is the Mid-Michigan Correctional Facility in St. Louis. **Secure Level VI** falls at the opposite end of the security level scale. Michigan has only one Secure Level VI prison, the Ionia Maximum Correctional Facility in Ionia. This prison houses offenders who are considered to be a constant security risk at other facilities and who pose maximum management problems for the MDOC. Some facilities may house more than one security level.[6]

During the 2002 fiscal year, the majority of offenders were placed in low security facilities. Approximately 67 percent were in Level I and Level II facilities. Levels III and IV housed approximately 17 percent of offenders, and almost 8 percent were housed in Levels V and VI. The remaining offenders were in reception, special centers, special use housing, or on electronic monitoring.[7]

The Cost of Incarceration in a State Prison

The cost of incarcerating an offender in a state facility depends on the custody level. During FY 2002, the average yearly cost of incarcerating one inmate was $24,680. Broken down by custody level, the average daily cost was:

- Level I $18,673
- Level II $19,052
- Level III $18,813
- Level IV $28,057
- Level V/VI $30,322
- Multi-level $21,834

These costs include not only the cost of supervising and housing inmates and providing programs and services, but also the indirect administrative costs for the DOC support of prison facilities.[8]

Prisoner Intake and Classification to Security Levels

When an inmate is transferred to the MDOC to begin serving a sentence of incarceration, s/he is first sent to a **reception and guidance center** for processing, evaluation, and classification. This process takes approximately ten days, although inmates may stay in the reception center for up to five weeks while waiting for a cell in their assigned prison facility to become available. There are two reception centers in Michigan, one for men and one for women. The male center, the Charles Egeler Reception and Guidance Center, is located in Jackson. It opened in July 2002 and consolidates three reception centers into one facility, significantly streamlining the intake process. Female offenders go through the intake procedure at the Robert Scott Correctional Facility in Plymouth.

An offender is brought to the reception center by the county sheriff's office. S/he first goes through an initial process of being fingerprinted and photographed. The offenders showers and is given prison clothing and a toiletry kit. While in the reception center the offender goes through a battery of tests, including

- a physical examination
- tests for HIV, TB, and venereal disease
- dental and eye examinations
- psychological testing, including the Minnesota Multi-phasic Personality Inventory
- educational testing to measure reading and math skills

After all tests are completed, a classification committee reviews the test results and other information about the inmate, including the presentence report. This committee will assign the inmate to a security level and a specific facility, based on the reports and test results. If the offender has special needs (e.g., a need for special protection or special programming), this will be taken into consideration when assigning the offender to a prison facility.[9]

PRISON LABOR IN MICHIGAN

A History of Prison Labor in Michigan

In 1843, Michigan instituted the **contract labor system** in the Jackson Prison. The system allowed private industry to manufacture products using cheap prison labor. The prison supplied the inmate labor and the building where the inmates worked. The private entrepreneur supplied machinery, supplies, and other equipment, and paid between $0.34 and $0.56 per day per inmate. These salaries were paid directly to the prison; the inmates did not receive any payment for their labor. Products manufactured by inmates during this period included shoes, harnesses, farm equipment, cotton and woolen items, carpeting, farm tools, steam engines, furniture, and barrels. In 1869, 517 of the 625 inmates at Jackson Prison were employed in some type of contract labor. However, by 1900 the system had been discontinued.[10]

In the early 20th century, Michigan began developing **prison industries**. This program eventually evolved into the current Michigan Prison Industries program. One of the earliest prison industries involved inmates producing license plates for the state. The first places were produced before 1910 and were made of leather, with metal house numbers. Jackson Prison first began producing license plates for automobiles in 1918. The same year, inmates also began making street and road signs for the state. In 1922, the state began to establish factories in various prison facilities, including a cement plant and a textile plant. Other products manufactured in state factories included bricks, tile, cigars, tombstones, and binder twine. Many of the products manufactured were for state use but products were also sold on the open market.[11]

In the 1920s and 1930s, several federal laws were passed to regulate prison industries. The 1935 **Hawes Cooper Act**[12] regulated interstate transportation of prison-made goods and the 1935 **Ashurst Summers Act**[13] provided criminal penalties for the interstate sale of prison-made products. The same year, the state passed the **Prison Industries Act**[14] to regulate inmate labor in prisons. The Act limited the sale of prison-made goods to state institutions and other agencies that were fully tax supported. In 1968, the Prison Industries Act was repealed, and replaced with the **Correctional Industries Act.**[15] In 1980, the Act was amended to allow the sale of prison-made products to non-profit organizations, governmental agencies in other states, federal government agencies, and foreign governments. Currently, MCL §800.326(1) states that,

> Correctional industries products may be sold, exchanged, or purchased by institutions of this or any other state or political subdivision of this or any other state, the federal government or agencies of the federal government, a foreign government or agencies of a foreign government, a private vendor that operates the youth correctional facility, or any organization that is a tax exempt organization under section 501©)(3) of the internal revenue code.

Prison Labor in Michigan Today

Many inmates in Michigan work at some job, although the majority work inside prison facilities. One goal of MDOC is to provide every able-bodied inmate with a meaningful work experience as a way of reducing crime, improving inmate self-sufficiency, and reducing prison management problems. Many inmates are employed by **Michigan State Industries** (MSI), a statewide program that administers prison industries in Michigan prison facilities. Inmates learn job skills that will help them obtain employment when released from prison. In 2000, MSI jobs provided incentive wages of between $.25 and $.90 per hour, depending on the skills of the inmate worker.[16]

There are a wide variety of work opportunities. Inmates at the Ionia Maximum Correctional Facility manufacture tables, chairs, and cushions, and perform furniture restoration. The Gus Harrison Correctional Facility houses a license plate factory. Marquette Branch Prison inmates operate a dairy facility and manufacture work garments of various types. Other products and services provided by MSI inmate employees include:

- janitorial products
- office furniture
- beds and mattresses for institutional use
- jail and prison furniture
- uniforms
- bed and bath linens
- laundry services for state prisons, hospitals, and some state agencies
- a variety of speciality products
- printing and duplicating services
- optical and dental laboratories
- a program to refurbish used computers for schools and non-profit organizations[17]

In addition to employment with MSI, some offenders may be given the opportunity to participate in community service and public works activities. Recent community service activities include:

- cleanup and maintenance of state parks and hiking trails
- cleanup of cemeteries
- washing police cars
- cleaning up vacant lots
- cleanup and maintenance of county fairgrounds
- painting and repairing houses for Habitat for Humanity

Work crews generally include eight to ten offenders who are supervised by correctional officers or in some cases by police officers.[18]

A public works assignment is "a supervised offender work assignment off Department grounds, sponsored by a qualified public or non-profit agency."[19] Only offenders housed in Security Level I facilities or Technical Rule Violation Centers are eligible. To participate in a public works assignment, offenders must meet a number of conditions, most of which relate to the offense for which the offender is serving a sentence of incarceration. Offenders serving a life sentence are not eligible for public works assignments.[20]

JAILS IN MICHIGAN

In Michigan, the primary difference between a **jail** and a **prison** is that prisons are run by the state whereas jails are managed by the county or local municipality. MCL §51.75 states that:

> The sheriff shall have the charge and custody of the jails of his county, and of the
> prisoners in the same; and shall keep them himself, or by his deputy or jailer.

The statute does not mandate a jail but it is clear from this and other statutes that counties are responsible for providing a local confinement facility. The sheriff is responsible for developing the rules and regulations governing prisoner conduct, although they must be approved by the county circuit court judge.[21]

The majority of inmates in county jails are pretrial detainees and convicted offenders serving short terms of incarceration, usually for misdemeanors. **Pretrial detainees** are defendants who are held in confinement while awaiting trial, generally because they do not satisfy the conditions of pretrial release that were set by the magistrate or judge. For example, a defendant's release order may require pretrial release upon payment of a specified amount of money (a bond). However, until the defendant is able to obtain the required amount of money, or arrange for a bail bondsman to secure the bond, s/he will be detained in the county jail.

The majority of **convicted offenders** in county jails are serving short terms of imprisonment. MCL §769.28 states that any individual sentenced to a term of imprisonment of no more than one year will serve the sentence in the county jail rather than in a state penal institution. However, a small number of offenders who have been sentenced to a term of incarceration to be served in a state prison may be held temporarily in a county jail until a space in a state prison becomes available.

In addition, some inmates may be confined in a county jail because of **contempt of court**. **Civil contempt** involves an individual failing to comply with a court order when s/he is capable of doing so. A person found in civil contempt by the court may be placed in a county jail until s/he is willing to comply with the court order. **Criminal contempt** involves deliberate disobedience of a court order or showing disrespect to the court during proceedings.

Oakland County Jail System

The **Oakland County Jail System** is the responsibility of the Oakland County Sheriff's Office (OCSO). The jail houses approximately 1,800 arrested suspects, pretrial detainees, and offenders sentenced to a term of incarceration of up to one year. The responsibility for the jail system is divided between two divisions of the OCSO. The **Corrective Services Division** supervises approximately 1,000 inmates in the county's **Main Jail** facility. The jail provides facilities for minimum, medium, and maximum security offenders. The Corrective Services Division is also responsible for supervising Booking Unit operations, inmate visitation, and all food services for inmates. In 2000, the Division privatized jail food services by entering into a contract with Aramark which saves the OCSO approximately $1.6 million annually. Another responsibility for the Correctional Services Division is community education. Over 100 jail tours are given annually. Some are for the general public while others are geared towards juveniles in the juvenile court system.[22]

The **Corrective Services Satellite Division** is responsible for all inmates not under the jurisdiction of the Corrective Services Division. The Division operates a **Regimented Inmate Discipline Program**, or **Boot Camp** which is an eight-week program for non-violent felony offenders that results in a sentence reduction upon successful completion. The boot camp provides a heavily-disciplined military-style environment that also includes substance abuse counseling, GED classes, physical fitness, training in employability skills, and community service activities. In 2000, the boot camp saved the state almost $1.5 million in jail days and provided community service to a variety of programs throughout the county.[23]

The Satellite Division also operates a **Trusty Camp** for low-level offenders who participate in a variety of community work projects. Projects include renovations to county buildings, road garbage pickup, and county park cleanup. The Division's **Work Release minimum security facility** houses inmates who are allowed to work in the community while serving their sentences. The facility houses 154 male and 24 female inmates who are charged room and board for their stay. In addition, the Satellite Division is under contract with the City of Southfield to operate the **Southfield Detention Facility**, which holds not only prisoners from Southfield but also most of the offenders arrested in Royal Oak Township. This jail has bed space for 68 permanent inmates as well as space for 12 inmates in holding tanks. Finally, the Satellite Division is responsible for the operation of the **Frank Greenan Detention Facility**. This jail is a 180-bed medium-security facility that was built in 1996 as a way of relieving overcrowding problems in the Main Jail. The facility operates a full-service laundry that provides laundry services for the Main Jail as well as a number of Satellite Division facilities.[24]

Wayne County Jail Division

As noted in Chapter 4, the **Wayne County Sheriff's Office** (WCSO) is the largest sheriff's department in Michigan. The **Jail Division** is the oldest division in the WCSO and includes three adult detention facilities. The **Andrew C. Baird Detention Facility** (also known as **Division One**) was completed in 1984. It is a 14-story building that includes bed space for 1,088 inmates, as well as 150 beds in the mental health unit and a 20-bed infirmary section. The facility also houses the central booking area and the county's jail classification system.[25]

The **Wayne County Jail**, also known as the "Old County Jail" or **Division Two** is the oldest jail facility in the county. It was constructed in 1929 and houses both sentenced offenders and pretrial detainees. The facility has space for 641 individuals.[26]

Division Three, the **William Dickerson Jail**, is the newest jail facility in Wayne County. It was completed in 1991 and houses 804 inmates in a direct supervision environment. The jail includes a laundry facility that provides laundry services for the entire jail division, as well as a food service program that provides food services for the jails, the county juvenile detention center, and other county facilities.[27]

COMMUNITY SUPERVISION IN MICHIGAN

The MDOC's Field Operations Administration (FOA) is responsible for all types of community-based corrections programs. These include probation, parole, electronic monitoring, various community residential programs for offenders nearing parole release date, boot camp, and technical rule violation centers. Community based programs are significantly more cost-effective than prison for low-risk offenders because the cost of supervising offenders in the community is significantly lower than the cost of prison incarceration. The average yearly cost of supervising an offender in prison in Michigan was $24,680 in fiscal year 2002 (the actual cost varied by the supervision level of the facility). In contrast, the yearly cost of supervising an offender on probation or parole was $1,839.19. In 2002, the FOA was supervising a total of 73,461 offenders (compared to the 49,489 offenders incarcerated in prisons and camps during that year). Of these, approximately 76 percent were on probation, 21 percent were on parole, 1.5 percent were in community residential programs, and the rest were in halfway houses or on electronic monitoring.[28]

Offenders placed on community supervision are supervised by trained agents, most of whom have college degrees in criminal justice or a related field. Most agents specialize in parolees, probationers, or offenders who are resident in corrections centers or on electronic monitoring, although some agents may supervise offenders in all three categories. Monitoring techniques include home visits, contact with law enforcement officials, contact with employers, confirming attendance at school or required programs, and substance abuse testing.[29]

Parole

Parole is not in itself a sentence. It is defined in Michigan as "a period of supervision and testing in the community prior to release from parole board jurisdiction."[30] The **Michigan Parole Board** is under the supervision of the FOA and is responsible for all felony offenders on parole in the state. The Board is also responsible for advising the governor on issues of clemency. In 2002, a total of 15,592 individuals were on parole in Michigan.[31]

In 1992, MCL §791.231a significantly reorganized the Parole Board. The Board consists of ten members, who may not be civil service employees. Members of the Board are appointed by the Director of the MDOC and serve four-year terms. The Board is divided into panels of three members and the parole decision is made by a majority vote of the panel. However, cases involving an offender sentenced to life in prison must be decided by a majority vote of the entire Board. If parole is denied, the offender will be given a date for the next Parole Board review.

MCL §791.233 outlines a number of limitations on granting parole to an offender. These include:

- the Board must be reasonably certain that the offender will not endanger the public safety or be a menace to society before releasing the offender on parole.

- the offender must have served the minimum term imposed by the court, minus any good time s/he has earned before being released on parole.

- the Board must have evidence that arrangements have been made for the offender's employment, education, or care upon release before releasing the offender on parole.

- if the offender was sentenced to a minimum term of two years incarceration, s/he must have earned a high school diploma or GED before being released on parole (this restriction may be waived under certain conditions outlined in the statute).

The Parole Board considers a number of factors when making parole decisions. These include:

- the offense for which the offender is incarcerated
- the offender's prior criminal record
- the offender's behavior in the institution
- the offender's participation in institutional programming
- information obtained from an interview with the offender
- information obtained from victims and other sources
- the parole guidelines score

The **parole guidelines score** is calculated based on the offenders current offense, prior record, institutional conduct and performance, age, mental status, and statistical risk classification. The purpose of the scoring system is to reduce disparity in the decision-making process as well as to increase the Board's efficiency.[32]

In 2002, the overall parole approval rate in Michigan was 48.4 percent.[33] However, this figure varies by the type of offense committed. Drug offenders had the highest approval rate; approximately 73 percent of drug offenders were approved for parole. Other nonviolent offenders had a 61 percent approval rate. At the other end of the spectrum, sex offenders had a 10 percent approval rate, while other violent offenders had a 35 percent approval rate.[34]

If parole is granted, the Board sets the length of the parole term and may impose a variety of conditions of parole. The offender must comply with these conditions or face revocation. Possible conditions of parole may include:

- the parolee must report to a parole officer regularly, must permit the officer to visit him or her at home or at other locations, and must allow himself or herself to be searched by a parole officer at reasonable times.
- the parolee may not move or change jobs without prior approval from a parole officer.

- the parolee must work or attend school/vocational training.
- the parolee must attend or live in a community residential home for parolees.
- the parolee must support dependents and meet family responsibilities.
- the parolee must pay restitution to the victim.
- the parolee must comply with the sex offenders registration act (if relevant).
- the parolee must not engage in any criminal behavior.
- the parolee may not possess a firearm.
- the parolee may not associate with any known criminals.

Conditions of parole are determined by the Board based on the offender's crime and personal background. Violations of parole conditions may result in a variety of punishments, including the imposition of more restrictions, community service, placement in a residential center, or return to prison.[35]

Probation

Unlike parole, **probation** is a sentence imposed by the court. The sentence is served in the community, rather than in a prison or jail, and the offender is supervised and required to abide by various conditions. In Michigan, probation may be imposed for any misdemeanor offense, and for many felonies as well. According to MCL §771.1(1),

> In all prosecutions for felonies or misdemeanors other than murder, treason, criminal sexual conduct in the first or third degree, armed robbery, and major controlled substance offenses ... if the defendant has been found guilty upon verdict or plea and the court determines that the defendant is not likely again to engage in an offensive or criminal course of conduct and that the public good does not require that the defendant suffer the penalty imposed by law, the court may place the defendant on probation under the charge and supervision of a probation officer.

In 2002, a total of 55,605 offenders were on probation in Michigan.[36]

MCL 771.2 outlines the maximum terms of probation that may be imposed by the court. In most cases, misdemeanor offenders are sentenced to a maximum of two years while felony offenders are sentenced to a period of no more than five years. However, offenders convicted of certain major drug offenses may be sentenced to life on probation.

Offenders placed on probation may be required to comply with a variety of conditions imposed by the court. These include both regular and special conditions. Regular conditions are imposed upon all probationers and include the following:

(a) During the term of his or her probation, the probationer shall not violate any criminal law of this state, the United States, or another state or any ordinance of any municipality in this state or another state.

(b) During the term of his or her probation, the probationer shall not leave the state without the consent of the court granting his or her application for probation.

(c) The probationer shall report to the probation officer, either in person or in writing, monthly or as often as the probation officer requires...

(d) If convicted of a felony, the probationer shall pay a probation supervision fee...

(e) The probationer shall pay restitution to the victim...

(f) The probationer shall pay an assessment...

(g) The probationer shall pay the minimum state cost...

(h) If the probationer is required to be registered under the sex offenders registration act ... the probationer shall comply with that act.[37]

In addition, the court has the option of imposing a variety of special conditions, depending on the circumstances of the case. Possible additional conditions may include:

(a) Be imprisoned in the county jail for not more than 12 months, at the time or intervals, which may be consecutive or nonconsecutive, within the probation as the court determines...

(b) Pay immediately or within the period of his or her probation a fine imposed when placed on probation.

(c) Pay costs...

(d) Pay any assessment ordered by the court...

(e) Engage in community service.

(f) Agree to pay by wage assignment any restitution, assessment, fine, or cost imposed by the court.

(g) Participate in inpatient or outpatient drug treatment.

(h) Participate in mental health treatment.

(i) Participate in mental health or substance abuse counseling.

(j) Participate in a community corrections program.

(k) Be under house arrest.

(l) Be subject to electronic monitoring.

(m) Participate in a residential probation program.

(n) Satisfactorily complete a program of incarceration in a special alternative incarceration unit...

(o) Be subject to conditions reasonably necessary for the protection of 1 or more named persons.

(p) Reimburse the county for expenses incurred by the county in connection with the conviction for which probation was ordered...[38]

Failure to comply with conditions of probation may result in a variety of sanctions, including revocation of probation.

Other Forms of Community Supervision

Another alternative to prison for some offenders is the **Special Incarceration Program** (SIP) or **boot camp** program.. The program includes three phases. Phase I lasts 90 days and is extremely regimented. Activities include military-style exercises, substance abuse treatment, and educational programming. Participants are also given work assignments. Recent work activities have included snow removal near senior citizen housing, park maintenance, and conservation work. Participants in Phase II live in a residential halfway house under intensive supervision for up to 120 days or are placed on electronic monitoring. Not all offenders are required to go through Phase II, participation depends on the offender's need (as assessed by the FOA) for a period of residential placement. In Phase III, offenders live in the community and experience basically the same level of supervision as a probationer. Phase III lasts for 18 months or the remainder of the offender's minimum sentence (whichever is longer). Phase III offenders are required to attend school or work for at least 30 hours per week, submit to random drug testing, and participate in assigned counseling, treatment, or training programs. The primary goal of the boot camp program is "to keep selected lower-risk probationers from going to prison and to take qualified prisoners out of the traditional prison setting and place them into a more cost-effective management setting."[39]

Some offenders in the community are placed on **electronic monitoring**, or the **electronic tether program**. Electronic monitoring allows significantly more intensive supervision of offenders. Using the system, the probation or parole officer can determine if the offender is at home or not. The system assists the officer in enforcing conditions of probation or parole, such as a curfew requirement. In most cases, offenders placed on electronic monitoring are supervised more closely and intensively than other offenders in the community.[40] In 2002, a total of 673 offenders were on electronic monitoring.[41]

The MDOC operates a number of **Technical Rule Violation (TRV) Centers**. TRV Centers are designed to house offenders who violate conditions of probation or parole, reducing the need to return these offenders to prison and thus helping to alleviate problems of prison crowding. The first TRV Center opened in 1991 in Lake County. Currently there are three TRV Centers, supervised by the FOA. Offenders who violate conditions of community release are generally confined to a TRV Center for 75 days. While there, offenders participate in education programs and substance abuse treatment, as well as working in the facility or on public works crews. Offenders who successfully complete the TRV program are returned to the community under intensive supervision. If the offender fails to complete the TRV program successfully, his or her parole or probation status is revoked and the offender is returned to prison.[42]

VICTIMS' RIGHTS

The Michigan **Crime Victim's Rights Act** (CVRA)[43] and the Declaration of Rights in the Michigan State Constitution[44] outline a variety of rights to which victims of crimes are entitled. Among these are the right to a variety of notifications. These include:

- the right to be notified of the offender's earliest parole eligibility date

- the right to be notified if the offender is transferred to a minimum security facility or camp
- the right to be notified of the offender's release to a community residential program (including electronic monitoring)
- the right to be notified of the offender's discharge (the MDOC sends this notification 90 days prior to the offender's discharge)
- the right to be notified of any public hearing regarding a reprieve, commutation, or pardon
- the right to be notified if a reprieve, commutation, or pardon is granted
- the right to be notified if the offender escapes from a MDOC facility (MDOC attempts to notify the victim by telephone within one hour of the escape and follows this up with a written notification as well)
- the right to submit a written statement to the parole board
- the right to be notified of the parole board decision
- the right to be notified if the offender is placed in a boot camp and when the offender is transferred to and from the boot camp
- the right to be notified if the offender legally changes his or her name while under MDOC jurisdiction.
- the right to be notified that the offender has been convicted of a new crime
- the right to be notified that the offender's parole was revoked[45]

As a way of more efficiently providing telephone notifications to victims of the unanticipated release of an offender, the MDOC participates in the **Michigan Crime Victim Notification Network**. Examples of unanticipated releases include a release on bond, a discharge by court order, or an escape. The Network may also notify victims about other changes in the offender's custody status. In addition, victims may also call the Network hotline to obtain information on an offender's current custody status.[46]

NOTES

1.   MCL §791.201 *et seq.* (PA 232 of 1953)
2.   MCL §791.302
3.   Michigan Department of Corrections home page (http://www.michigan.gov/corrections)
4.   Michigan Department of Corrections (2003). *Annual Report: 2002.* (http://www.state.mi.us/mdoc/jobs/pdfs/2002AnnualReport.pdf)
5.   *Ibid*
6.   Michigan Department of Corrections home page, *op. cit.*
7.   Michigan Department of Corrections (2003). *Annual Report: 2002. op. cit.*
8.   *Ibid*
9.   Michigan Department of Corrections home page, *op. cit.*
10.   Michigan State Industries home page (http://www.michigan.gov/msi)
11.   *Ibid*

12.   49 U.S.C. §11507
13.   18 U.S.C. §1761
14.   MCL §800.301- 800.319
15.   MCL §800.321 *et seq.*
16.   Michigan Department of Corrections (2001). *2000 Statistical Report.* (http://www.michigan.gov/documents/Stat2000_51449_7.pdf)
17.   Michigan State Industries home page, *op. cit.*
18.   Michigan Department of Corrections home page, *op. cit.*
19.   *Ibid*
20.   *Ibid*
21.   MCL §51.281
22.   Oakland County Sheriff's Office home page (http://www.co.oakland.mi.us/sheriff/)
23.   *Ibid*
24.   *Ibid*
25.   Wayne County Sheriff's Office home page (http://www.waynecounty.com/default_gov.htm)
26.   *Ibid*
27.   *Ibid*
28.   Michigan Department of Corrections (2003). *Annual Report: 2002. op. cit.*
29.   Michigan Department of Corrections home page, *op. cit.*
30.   *Ibid*
31.   Michigan Department of Corrections (2003). *Annual Report: 2002. op. cit.*
32.   Michigan Department of Corrections home page, *op. cit.*
33.   Michigan Department of Corrections (2003). *Annual Report: 2002. op. cit.*
34.   Michigan Department of Corrections home page, *op. cit.*
35.   *Ibid*
36.   Michigan Department of Corrections (2003). *Annual Report: 2002. op. cit.*
37.   MCL §771.3(1)
38.   MCL §771.3(2)
39.   Michigan Department of Corrections home page, *op. cit.*
40.   *Ibid*
41.   Michigan Department of Corrections (2003). *Annual Report: 2002. op. cit.*
42.   Michigan Department of Corrections home page, *op. cit.*
43.   MCL §780.751 *et seq.*
44.   Michigan State Constitution, Article I, §24
45.   Michigan Department of Corrections home page, *op. cit.*
46.   *Ibid*

CHAPTER 9

THE JUVENILE JUSTICE SYSTEM
IN MICHIGAN

INTRODUCTION

In Michigan, cases involving **juveniles** fall under the family division of the circuit court. A juvenile is an individual under the age of 17. The court has jurisdiction over juvenile delinquents who fall into one of three categories:

1. The juvenile is accused of committing an offense that would be considered a crime if committed by an adult.

2. The juvenile is accused of committing a **status offense**. A status offense is an age-based offense, an act that is only considered to be a crime when it is committed by a juvenile (e.g., violation of juvenile curfew, truancy, running away from home).

3. The juvenile is accused of being a "wayward minor" - being engaged in non-criminal activities that are dangerous to the juvenile's health, safety, or morals.[1]

The family division of the circuit court also has jurisdiction over child protective proceedings and cases involving minors who have been charged with misdemeanor traffic violations.[2]

THE JUVENILE JUSTICE PROCESS IN MICHIGAN

The juvenile justice system differs in several key ways from the adult criminal justice system. After a juvenile is taken into custody by the police, s/he is required to appear in the family division of circuit court for a **preliminary inquiry**. The purpose of this proceeding is for the court to determine if there is sufficient probable cause to continue with the case. The court has several options at this inquiry. First, the case may be dismissed for lack of probable cause. Second, the juvenile may be **diverted** into a public or private diversion program. Third, a formal **petition** may be filed.

In some cases, the court may decide to divert the juvenile into a **juvenile diversion program**. Diversion occurs when:

a formally recorded apprehension is made by a law enforcement agency for an act by a minor that if a petition were filed with the court would bring that minor within... section 712A.2 of the Michigan Compiled Laws, and instead of petitioning the court or authorizing a petition, either of the following occurs:

    (i) The minor is released into the custody of his or her parent, guardian, or custodian and the investigation is discontinued.

    (ii) The minor and the minor's parent, guardian, or custodian agree to work with a person or public or private organization or agency that will assist the minor and the minor's family in resolving the problem that initiated the investigation.[3]

Participation in a diversion program is always voluntary. One example of a juvenile diversion program is that run by the **Alger/Schoolcraft Family Court**. The program focuses on all first-time status offenders and all first-time less serious juvenile delinquent offenders. The program intake counselors are given discretion in determining who is eligible for admission into the program.[4] A number of factors must be considered when deciding whether to divert a minor, including:

    (a) The nature of the alleged offense.
    (b) The minor's age.
    (c) The nature of the problem that led to the alleged offense.
    (d) The minor's character and conduct.
    (e) The minor's behavior in school, family, and group settings.
    (f) Any prior diversion decisions made concerning the minor and the nature of the minor's compliance with the diversion agreement.[5]

The diversion program generally lasts for three months, although the caseworker assigned to a particular juvenile may set the case for a longer or shorter period of diversion. The caseworker will develop a diversionary agreement with the juvenile. This agreement may include any or all of the following:

- requiring the juvenile to make restitution
- requiring the juvenile to perform community service
- requiring the juvenile to observe a curfew
- requiring the juvenile to participate in substance abuse and/or mental health counseling
- requiring the juvenile to obey his or her parents

If the juvenile fails to comply with the diversion agreement, the period of diversion may be extended beyond the original 90-day period or a petition may be filed and the juvenile formally processed through the juvenile justice system.[6]

If the juvenile is not diverted from formal proceedings, or if the juvenile fails to complete a diversion agreement, a formal **petition** is filed with the court by the prosecuting attorney.[7] The court will schedule a **preliminary hearing**. At this hearing, the juvenile is formally informed of the allegations outlined in the petition filed with the court and is advised of his or her rights. These include the right to an attorney, the right to a trial by judge or jury, and the protection against self-incrimination. The juvenile is also given the opportunity to plead to the allegations in the petition.[8] The court may at this time appoint an attorney to represent the juvenile in any of the following situations:

- the juvenile's parents refuse to appear and participate in the delinquency proceedings

- the parent is the victim or complainant in the case

- the juvenile's family cannot afford to hire an attorney

- the court considers it to be in the best interests of the juvenile and public to require an attorney be appointed (and the juvenile does not waive his or her right to an attorney).[9]

The court must also decide whether to retain the juvenile in custody until the trial. Juveniles who are detained by the court are usually placed in a juvenile detention center. However, in some cases, a juvenile may be held in an adult jail. In these cases, the juvenile must be kept separate from the adults incarcerated in the facility. According to MCR Rule 3.935(D), the court may only detain a juvenile if:

> The court finds probable cause to believe the juvenile committed the offense, and that one or more of the following circumstances are present:
> (a) the offense alleged is so serious that release would endanger the public safety;
> (b) the juvenile is charged with an offense that would be a felony if committed by an adult and will likely commit another offense pending trial, if released, and
> (i) another petition is pending against the juvenile,
> (ii) the juvenile is on probation, or
> (iii) the juvenile has a prior adjudication but is not under the court's jurisdiction at the time of apprehension;
> (c) there is a substantial likelihood that if the juvenile is released to the parent, guardian, or legal custodian, with or without conditions, the juvenile will fail to appear at the next court proceeding;
> (d) the home conditions of the juvenile make detention necessary;
> (e) the juvenile has run away from home;
> (f) the juvenile has failed to remain in a detention facility or nonsecure facility or placement in violation of a valid court order; or
> (a) pretrial detention is otherwise specifically authorized by law.

If the court decides not to detain the juvenile prior to trial, s/he may be released to the custody of a parent or guardian. The court has the option of imposing conditions on the release as a means of ensuring that the juvenile will appear in court when required and/or as a way of reasonably ensuring the public safety. Conditions that may be imposed on a juvenile released prior to trial include, but are not limited to:

- the juvenile must not commit any offense
- the juvenile must not use alcohol, tobacco, or any controlled substance
- the juvenile must participate in a substance abuse treatment program
- the juvenile must comply with stated restrictions regarding where s/he lives
- the juvenile must comply with stated restrictions regarding who s/he associates with
- the juvenile must obey a stated curfew
- the juvenile must attend school
- the juvenile must surrender his or her driver's license

If the juvenile violates any condition of release, the court may order the juvenile to be detained and may revoke his or her pretrial release status.[10] The court may also require the juvenile's parent or guardian to post bail as a condition of the juvenile's release.[11]

The family division of the circuit court may also decide to **waive jurisdiction** over the juvenile and transfer the case to the adult criminal court. A waiver of jurisdiction may only occur if the juvenile is at least fourteen years of age and is accused of what would, if committed by an adult, be considered a felony offense.[12] Juveniles transferred to adult criminal court are given all the constitutional rights of any adult offender.

If the juvenile is not transferred to adult court, s/he will proceed to the **trial**. The purpose of this proceeding is to determine whether the allegations made against the juvenile are true. The level of proof required in a juvenile trial is the same as that required in an adult trial: proof beyond a reasonable doubt. The trial must be held within six months after the filing of the petition, unless there is good cause for a delay. The juvenile has the right to be present at the trial, along with his or her parents, guardian ad litem, and attorney. In addition, any victims have the right to be present at trial.[13] However, if the victim is going to be called as a witness, the court does have the option of ordering the victim sequestered until after s/he testifies.[14]

The procedures for a juvenile trial are similar to that of a trial in adult criminal court, with the district attorney presenting evidence against the juvenile and the juvenile's lawyer presenting evidence in the juvenile's defense. If the court finds that the allegations set forth in the petition were not proved beyond a reasonable doubt, the juvenile is immediately released from custody (if s/he was being held in custody prior to trial) and is no longer under the jurisdiction of the juvenile justice system. However, if the court finds that the allegations have been proved, the juvenile is adjudicated to be delinquent and may be held in custody while awaiting **disposition** of the case.

If a juvenile is adjudicated delinquent, the court may order a **predisposition investigation** to be conducted. In most cases, the predisposition investigation, which is similar to the presentence investigation conducted in the adult criminal court, is carried out by juvenile probation officers in the employ of the family division of the circuit court. The final report is known as a **predisposition report** and may not be considered by the court until after adjudication. The report generally includes a risk and needs assessment that contains information on the juvenile's social history, educational background, medical and psychological condition, as well as information on factors relating to the likelihood of recidivism.

After the completion of the predisposition report, the court will schedule a **dispositional hearing**. According to MCR Rule 3.943(A),

> A dispositional hearing is conducted to determine what measures the court will take with respect to a juvenile and, when applicable, any other person, once the court has determined following trial or plea that the juvenile has committed an offense.

There are a number of possible dispositional options or alternatives available to the court when dealing with a delinquent juvenile. The court selects the option that is most likely to protect the public, to meet the needs of the juvenile, and to be in the juvenile's best interests. MCL §712A.18 lists a variety of possible dispositional alternatives. Examples include various types of custodial and non-custodial supervision; requiring the juvenile to perform community service, pay a civil fine, pay court costs, or make restitution; and requiring the juvenile to participate in a juvenile boot camp.

THE MICHIGAN BUREAU OF JUVENILE JUSTICE

The Michigan **Family Independence Agency** (FIA) oversees a variety of public assistance programs, including child and family welfare. One of the many specialized programs within the FIA is the **Bureau of Juvenile Justice** (BJJ). The BJJ provides social services for juvenile delinquents between the ages of 12 and 20 who have been referred to the FIA by the courts. Services include crime prevention, rehabilitation, and correctional programs.[15]

The BJJ operates seven residential facilities for delinquent juveniles. These range from low-security facilities such as the Arbor Heights Center in Ann Arbor to high security facilities like the W.J. Maxey Training School in Whitmore Lake. These facilities provide treatment, education, and recreational programs for juveniles. In addition, BJJ operates five community justice centers that provide educational services and skill training for juveniles who are re-entering the community. Home-based surveillance programs, such as electronic monitoring, are also provided, in an attempt to prevent juveniles from being placed outside the home.[16]

In 1998, the BJJ began to employ the **Balanced and Restorative Justice** (BARJ) philosophy. Restorative justice is a social movement that stresses healing over retribution. A crime causes injury to the victim, to the community, and to the offender; according to the restorative justice philosophy, the criminal justice process should help to repair those injuries. Restorative justice emphasizes the act committed by the delinquent, and the harm that is caused by this act. A basic tenet is offender accountability: the juvenile must acknowledge the harm resulting from his or her actions and must attempt to repair that harm, at least as much as possible. In return, the community is obligated to give the offender the opportunity to restore the victim to his or her pre-victimization state and must try to reintegrate the juvenile back into the community at the end of this process. Restorative justice emphasizes the needs of the victim and encourages victim participation in determining case outcomes. It also addresses the needs of the juvenile offender and emphasizes healing, rehabilitation, and reintegration over incapacitation and removal from the community. Restorative justice programs include mediation, arbitration, victim advocacy, conflict and dispute resolution, and consensus building.

THE MICHIGAN DEPARTMENT OF CORRECTIONS

If the family division of the circuit court has waived jurisdiction over a juvenile, s/he is tried in adult criminal court. If convicted, this juvenile is the responsibility of the MDOC. The majority of these juveniles are placed in boot camps. In 1999, the **Michigan Youth Correctional Facility** was opened near Baldwin. It is operated at security Level V and is run by contract with Wackenhut Corrections Corporation and houses male offenders under the age of 20 who have been convicted of a violent crime. The facility provides educational and vocational training, work assignments, and treatment programs such as Alcoholics Anonymous and Narcotics Anonymous.

NOTES

1. MCL §712A.2(a)
2. Michigan Courts home page (http://courts.michigan.gov/index.htm)
3. MCL §722.822(C)
4. Alger/Schoolcraft Family Court Juvenile Diversion Program (http://www.asprobate.org/diversion.pdf)
5. MCL §722.824
6. Alger/Schoolcraft Family Court Juvenile Diversion Program, *op cit.*
7. MCL §712A.11(2)
8. MCR Rule 3.935(B)
9. MCR Rule 3.915
10. MCR Rule 3.935(E)
11. MCR Rule 3.935(F)
12. MCL §712A.4
13. MCR Rule 3.942
14. MCL §780.761
15. Family Independence Agency home page (http://www.michigan.gov/fia)
16. *Ibid*

CHAPTER 10

DRUGS AND CRIME IN MICHIGAN

INTRODUCTION

Drug abuse is a serious problem in Michigan. During 2001, there were 43,501 narcotic law offenses and 34,803 narcotic law arrests reported to the Michigan Uniform Crime Reporting program. Of those offenders arrested, approximately 94 percent were adults. Approximately 85 percent of arrested offenders were male and 15 percent female.[1] The U.S. Drug Enforcement Administration (DEA) made an additional 511 arrests for drug law violations in the state. Federal drug violation arrests have been decreasing since 1997.[2]

THE AVAILABILITY OF DRUGS IN MICHIGAN

Marijuana

According to the DEA, **marijuana** is the most readily available and commonly used drug in Michigan. The majority is transported into the state after being smuggled across the U.S./Mexican border. However, marijuana is also grown in Michigan for local use as well as for export to other states and to Canada. Marijuana is also grown in Ontario by individuals of Vietnamese descent and smuggled across the boarder into Michigan.[3] A recent report on drug abuse in Detroit and surrounding Wayne County found that Mexican marijuana was the most common type available in the area.[4]

Cocaine

Cocaine, which is grown in Bolivia, Colombia, and Peru, is easily available in Michigan. It is frequently smuggled into the United States from Mexico and transported to Michigan by couriers. The DEA considers cocaine to be one of Michigan's most serious drug problems. Over the past few years, the price and purity of the drug has remained fairly stable. In general, a gram sells for between $75 and $125; an ounce sells for $500 to $1,300, and a kilogram of cocaine has a street value of $23,000 to $25,000. The cocaine sold in urban areas is generally between 80 and 90 percent pure.[5] In Detroit, a rock of crack typically costs between $5 and $50.[6]

In 2001, cocaine and crack cocaine were the main illegally abused drugs among individuals admitted to state-funded treatment programs in Michigan, representing 18 percent of total admissions.[7]

117

Heroin

Heroin is primarily found in urban areas in Michigan, including Detroit and other large cities. The majority of heroin that is available in Michigan is imported from Mexico, South America, and Africa, although heroin from Asia also is frequently found in the Detroit area.[8] The street price of heroin has remained fairly stable in the Detroit area over the past few years. A packet or "hit" generally costs $10 in Detroit, but may cost up to $15 in other parts of the state. Heroin purity averaged 43 percent in 2001.[9]

In 2001, heroin was the primary illegally abused drug among individuals admitted to state-funded treatment programs in Detroit and Wayne County, accounting for 34 percent of the total admissions, as well as 14 percent of admissions statewide. Deaths due to heroin has been increasing in the Detroit area since 1992; the number almost doubled between 1996 and 2000.[10]

Methamphetamine

According to the DEA, **methamphetamine** abuse is found most commonly in the western, southwestern, and central portions of Michigan. It is much less readily available in the Detroit area. The drug is produced in clandestine laboratories, primarily located in rural areas.[11]

Club Drugs

Club drugs include a number of illegal drugs that are found at nightclubs and "raves". Common club drugs in Michigan include MDMA (Ecstacy), GHB (gamma hydroxybutyric acid), and Ketamine. These drugs are becoming more popular among juveniles and young adults, especially those living in urban areas. The DEA notes that large seizures of MDMA occur regularly at Detroit Metropolitan Airport and at Detroit area ports of entry.[12]

MDMA use has been increasing in Michigan. Primary sources of MDMA include Canada and Western Europe. Canadian pills may be obtained for as little as $10 each, in lots of 500 or more. Ketamine use is also increasing, and there have been a number of burglaries of veterinary clinics in attempts to obtain the drug.[13]

THE DEA IN MICHIGAN

The DEA has offices located in Detroit, East Lansing, Grand Rapids, and Saginaw. During 2002, federal drug seizures in Michigan seized 12 kilograms of cocaine, 4.6 kilograms of heroin, and 529 kilograms of marijuana. In addition, during 2002, the DEA, along with state and local authorities, seized 233 clandestine laboratories.[14]

In 1997, law enforcement agencies in the Detroit area asked the Office of National Drug Control Policy to designate the area a High Intensity Drug Trafficking Area (HIDTA). The Michigan HIDTA is made up of nine counties and includes the cities of Detroit, Grand Rapids, Flint, and

Kalamzoo. It currently covers an area that accounts for approximately 50 percent of the state population.[15]

MICHIGAN DRUG TREATMENT COURTS

Drug courts are designed as a way to divert nonviolent drug and alcohol offenders out of traditional criminal justice prosecution. They handle cases involving offenders whose crimes are related to substance abuse through the use of extensive supervision and treatment. They also attempt to increase the coordination of various agencies and resources available to drug abusers, increase the cost-effectiveness of the programs, and provide the offender with access to a wide variety of programs and resources, with the goal of reducing recidivism and substance abuse among these offenders.

Michigan has been operating drug courts since 1992.[16] As of September 15, 2003, there were 30 active drug courts in Michigan, including nine that had been in operation for at least two years and 21 that were recent implemented. An additional 20 drug courts were in the planning stages. These include both adult and juvenile drug courts.[17]

To qualify for participation in most drug court programs in Michigan, an individual must meet certain general criteria. The individual must be addicted to a chemical substance, must be willing to volunteer for the program, and, in most cases, must be accused of a non-violent crime. Each program may have specific criteria excluding certain types of offenders. Individuals referred to the program generally go through an intensive screening process that includes the collection of information about the defendant's prior and current substance use and abuse as well as information about the defendant's criminal history. First offenders may be considered for admission into the program but the majority of participants are multiple offenders who have been through traditional treatment programs but are continuing to reappear in the criminal justice system.

Drug courts emphasize diversion, probation, and community control. The idea is to divert drug offenders from trial by providing alternatives to traditional criminal justice prosecution for drug-related offenses. Offenders generally must attend regular drug court sessions and comply with a variety of court-mandated educational, treatment, and rehabilitation requirements. These may include weekly treatment meetings, attendance at weekly 12-step meetings (e.g., Alcoholics Anonymous, Narcotics Anonymous), compliance with random drug tests, regular home and office visits with a probation officer, anger management classes, GED or literacy classes, participation in vocational rehabilitation, and abstinence from alcohol and other drugs.

If a program participant tests negative for drugs and attends the requirement meetings and treatment programs for a prescribed period of time, the treatment plan will be modified by reducing the requirements. Participants are also provided with referrals to various vocational, academic, and health-related programs. If participants do not make adequate progress, the judge may require them to participate in a residential treatment program or send them to jail for a period of time. Offenders may leave the drug court program voluntarily or by failing to comply with the rules of the program. For example, an offender who is found to be using drugs or who is charged with a new crime while in the drug court program may be terminated from the program.

Drug courts are an economical alternative for the state. It costs approximately $3,000 to $5,000 to maintain an offender in a drug court program, as compared to almost $30,000 per year to maintain an offender in prison. Currently, the recidivism rate for individuals who successfully complete the program is 13 percent.[18]

Oakland County runs a juvenile drug treatment court known as **Options: The Power to Choose**. To qualify for participation in the program, juveniles must be non-violent repeat offenders charged with a drug or alcohol offense, or a related crime. Juveniles accepted into the program attend weekly drug court sessions, submit to frequent random drug tests, attend regular probationary counseling sessions, and participate in AA or NA meetings. Rewards for positive performance include significant public praise in court by the judge. In addition, juveniles are rewarded with increased freedom, gift certificates, and field trips. Failure to comply with program requirements may result in the assignment of a curfew, community service hours, loss of privileges, home detention, or a short period of incarceration.[19]

NOTES

1.   Michigan State Police (2002). *Crime in Michigan: 2001 Uniform Crime Report*. (http://www.michigan.gov/documents/2001_UCR_Annual_Report_49321_7.pdf)
2.   Office of National Drug Control Policy, Drug Policy Information Clearinghouse (May, 2003). *State of Michigan: Profile of Drug Indicators*. (http://www.whitehousedrugpolicy.gov/statelocal/mi/mi.pdf)
3.   DEA Fact Sheet: *Michigan* (http://www.usdoj.gov/dea/pubs/states/michigan.html)
4.   Michigan Department of Community Health (2002). *Drug Abuse Trend Report, Wayne County, Michigan June 2002* (http://www.michigan.gov/documents/DrugTrends12-01_9374_7.PDF)
5.   DEA Fact Sheet: *Michigan, op cit.*
6.   Michigan Department of Community Health (2002). *op cit.*
7.   *Ibid*
8.   DEA Fact Sheet: *Michigan, op cit.*
9.   Michigan Department of Community Health (2002). *op cit.*
10.   *Ibid*
11.   DEA Fact Sheet: *Michigan, op cit.*
12.   *Ibid*
13.   Michigan Department of Community Health (2002). *op cit.*
14.   DEA Fact Sheet: *Michigan, op cit.*
15.   *Ibid*
16.   Range, Stacy (2003). "Michigan planning on expanding drug courts." *Lansing State Journal*, June 18. (http://www.lsj.com/news/capitol/030618courts_1a-8a.html)

17. American University School of Public Affairs (2003). *OJP Drug Court Clearinghouse and Technical Assistance Project: Summary of Drug Court Activity by State and County, September 15, 2003.* (http://www.american.edu/academic.depts/spa/justice/publications/drgchart2k.pdf)

18. Range, *op cit.*

19. Oakland County, Michigan home page - Family Focused Juvenile Drug Treatment Court (http://www.co.oakland.mi.us/circuit/program_service/options.html)

APPENDIX

WEB SITES OF INTEREST

There is a wealth of information on Michigan and the Michigan criminal justice system available on the world wide web. Below are a selection of web sites that may be of interest to students.

GENERAL MICHIGAN WEB SITES

http://www.michigan.gov/
> The official home page of the State of Michigan. It provides a variety of information services for citizens regarding Michigan history, government, and much more.

http://www.michigan.gov/emi/0,1303,7-102-116_355-2838--,00.html
> This provides a link to the *Michigan Manual*, the official manual of the State of Michigan. It includes information on the history of the state, the state constitution, state and local government, and statistics about the state. This page may also be accessed directly from the state's official home page.

http://www.michiganinbrief.org/edition07/About_files/MIB_2002.pdf
> This pdf file includes the entire text of the 7th edition of *Michigan in Brief: 2002-03*

http://www.michigan.gov/emi/0,1303,7-102-116_355---,00.html
> The official home page of the Michigan Legislature. It includes links to both the Senate and the House of Representatives. This page may also be accessed directly from the state's official home page.

http://www.michigan.gov/emi/0,1303,7-102-116_353---,00.html
> This page provides links to information about the executive branch, including the Office of the Governor, the Office of the Lieutenant Governor, and links to various State Departments and Agencies. This page may also be accessed directly from the state's official home page.

http://www.mivictims.org/index.html
> The home page of the Michigan Crime Victim's Website.

http://courts.michigan.gov/mji/resources/cvr/cvr.htm
> The Michigan Crime Victim Rights Manual.

http://www.michigan.gov/mdcr/0,1607,7-138-4956_5002---,00.html
 The home page of the Michigan Alliance Against Hate Crimes. This page may also be accessed directly from the state's official home page.

LEGAL INFORMATION

http://www.michiganlegislature.org/law/mileg.asp?page=ChapterIndex
 This link provides access to the Michigan Compiled Laws. Statutes may be searched by keyword for specific subjects of interest. The text of the Michigan State Constitution is located in Chapter 1 of the Michigan Compiled laws.

http://courtofappeals.mijud.net/rules/public/default.asp
 This link provides access to Michigan Court Rules.

http://courtofappeals.mijud.net/digest/topiclists/headingindex.htm
 This link accesses topics in the Michigan Appellate Digest.

http://www.courts.michigan.gov/mji/resources/sentencing-guidelines/sg.htm
 The State of Michigan Sentencing Guidelines Manual.

POLICE IN MICHIGAN

http://www.michigan.gov/msp
 The home page of the Michigan State Police.

http://www.michigan.gov/msp/1,1607,7-123-1593_3510---,00.html
 The home page of the Michigan Commission of Law Enforcement Standards. This page may also be accessed directly from the state's official home page.

http://www.ci.detroit.mi.us/police/default.htm
 The home page of the Detroit Police Department.

http://www.lansingpolice.com/
 The home page of the Lansing Police Department.

http://www.waynecounty.com/default_gov.htm
 The home page of Wayne County, MI. Information on the Wayne County Sheriff's Office may be accessed from this page.

http://www.co.oakland.mi.us/sheriff/
 The home page of the Oakland County Sheriff's Office.

http://www.ferris.edu/education/michiganpolicecorps/homepage.htm
    The home page of the Michigan Police Corps.

THE MICHIGAN COURT SYSTEM

http://www.courts.michigan.gov/
    The home page of the Michigan Courts.

http://www.michigan.gov/emi/0,1303,7-102-116_354---,00.html
    Links to the Michigan Courts. This page may also be accessed directly from the state's official home page.

http://www.michbar.org/
    The home page of the State Bar of Michigan.

CORRECTIONS IN MICHIGAN

http://www.michigan.gov/corrections
    The home page of the Michigan Department of Corrections.

http://www.state.mi.us/mdoc/jobs/pdfs/2002AnnualReport.pdf
    The Michigan Department of Corrections 2002 Annual Report.

http://www.michigan.gov/msi
    The home page of Michigan State Industries.

http://www.kalcounty.com/sheriff/jail.htm
    The home page of the Kalamazoo County Jail.

THE MICHIGAN JUVENILE JUSTICE SYSTEM

http://www.ncjj.org/stateprofiles/profiles/MI02.asp?state=MI02.asp&topic=Profile
    Information on state juvenile justice policies in Michigan.

http://www.michigan.gov/fia/0,1607,7-124-5452_7121_7198-15630--,00.html
    The home page of the Michigan Bureau of Juvenile Justice.

http://www.juvjus.state.nc.us/
    The home page of the Michigan Department of Juvenile Justice and Delinquency Prevention. This page may also be accessed directly from the state's official home page.

DRUGS IN MICHIGAN

http://www.whitehousedrugpolicy.gov/statelocal/mi/mi.pdf
> The Office of National Drug Control Policy provides a large amount of information on drug use statistics and drug prevention efforts in Michigan.

http://www.usdoj.gov/dea/pubs/states/michigan.html
> The Drug Enforcement Agency has fact sheets on every state in the U.S.

http://www.michigan.gov/documents/DrugTrends12-01_9374_7.PDF
> A 2002 report on drug abuse in Detroit and Wayne County.

http://courts.michigan.gov/scao/projects/spec.htm
> Information on drug courts in Michigan.

http://www.co.oakland.mi.us/circuit/program_service/options.html
> The home page of the Family Focused Juvenile Drug Treatment Court in Oakland County.